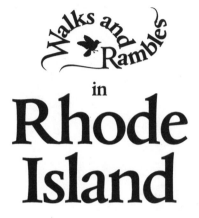

in

Rhode
Island

A park naturalist looks over relics of one of Beavertail Point's many shipwrecks.

in

Rhode Island

A guide to the natural and historic wonders of the ocean state

SECOND EDITION

KEN WEBER

Backcountry Publications
Woodstock · Vermont

An Invitation to the Reader

If you find that conditions have changed along these walks, please let the author and publisher know so that corrections may be made in future printings. Address all correspondence to:

Editor
Walks and Rambles Series
Backcountry Publications
P.O. Box 175
Woodstock, VT 05091

Library of Congress Cataloging-in-Publication Data

Weber, Ken.
Walks & rambles in Rhode Island : a guide to the natural & historic wonders of the Ocean State / Ken Weber. —2nd ed.
p.   cm.
ISBN 0-88150-261-8
1. Hiking—Rhode Island—Guidebooks.   2. Rhode Island—Guidebooks.
I. Title.   II. Title: Walks and rambles in Rhode Island.
GV199.42.R4W44   1993
917.45'0443—dc20   92–42203
                                                                          CIP

Published by Backcountry Publications
A division of The Countryman Press, Inc.
Woodstock, Vermont 05091
Printed in the United States of America

Design by Ann Aspell
Maps and calligraphy by Alex Wallach
Photographs by the author

For Bettie, my favorite companion on the trails. Through her, I learned how much more interesting, more memorable, each walk becomes when shared with somebody special.

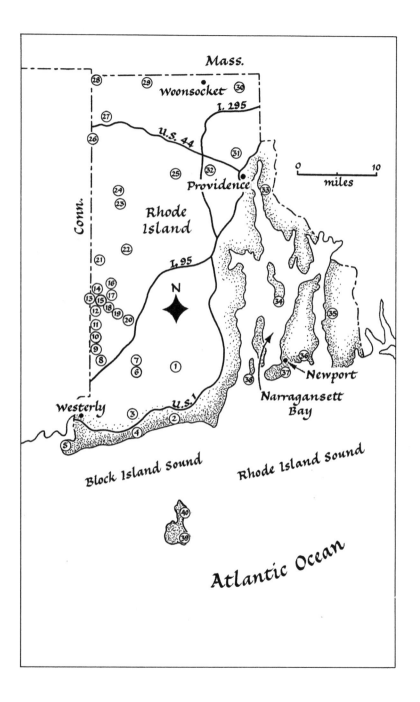

Contents

Introduction

Nothing stays the same—not even places to walk. Landmark trees fall in time; storms reshape the landscape; logged areas return to forest; and, inevitably, humans leave their mark: sometimes by improving trail systems, sometimes by causing paths to deteriorate, sometimes by merely changing path names. All in all, the result is that hiking guides need updating.

This second edition of *Walks & Rambles in Rhode Island* brings the 40 walking places up to date, noting many of the changes that have taken place since the original version was published in 1986. That book grew out of a need to update an earlier guide called *25 Walks in Rhode Island* that was published in 1978.

For the past year I've been rewalking these trails to detail the changes. Many are as simple as a change in names—the Burlingame Park Trail is now the Vin Gormley Trail, for example—and in some cases it's merely a matter of blazes that were painted a different color or a parking area that was moved slightly. Other changes, however, are highly significant. The Arcadia Trail, part of the Appalachian Mountain Club trail network, has been rerouted considerably; it starts at a different place and is now several miles longer than the previous trail. I've also devised a virtually all-new loop through the Black Hut Management Area because of problems created when the former trail crossed private property.

Even now the changes are continuing. Plans that could alter the walking of the Trestle Trail and the loop through the south part of Prudence Island are in the works. Nothing stays the same.

Yet these changes are more positive than negative. They mean that walking the trails never becomes stale. Time and again over the last year, when rewalking paths I've been on a dozen times, I found myself marveling over rock ledges or tranquil little ponds or surging young pine groves—all features that were present years ago but now look different, either because they have changed or because their surroundings have changed.

The walks are arranged geographically, starting with one of the state's most special places—the Great Swamp—then going clockwise around the southwestern, western, northern, and eastern areas before finally concluding with another unique spot: Block Island. In between are the beaches of Ninigret and Napatree, the vast forests along the western border, the quiet woods and fields in the northwestern corner, the rocky bluffs of Diamond Hill, the close-to-the-city parks of Lincoln Woods and Dame Farm, the wildlife sanctuaries and islands of Narragansett Bay, and the famed Cliff Walk in Newport.

Most of the walks are loops that enable you to return to the point where you began. Some, however, are one-way walks, making it necessary to leave another car at your terminus unless you plan to retrace your steps. It is important that you read the descriptions before starting out in order to best prepare yourself. The descriptions tell you whether to bring lunch, what to wear, how much time to allow, and so forth.

Each trail description provides distances and approximate walking times, along with notes about the trail's difficulty and, usually, the best time of year for choosing specific trails. It is often possible to link trails and do more than one in an outing, and information about where trails connect is included.

Walking times are based on my own pace, which is fairly brisk but with numerous stops at places of interest. Many experienced hikers could do these walks in far less time, but I don't consider walking a competitive sport or an endurance event. Those who plunge through the woods—never stopping, looking neither left nor right—miss far too much. There is so much beauty, history, and wildlife along these routes—it would be a shame not to see as much as possible.

Sketch maps of each walk are included to help you visualize the described route. The following standard map symbols are used:

℗	parking area
• • • •	main trail
. . . .	side trail or alternate route
X	point of interest
⬚	fields
⚘ ⚘	marsh
■	building
⊨	bridge
†	cemetery
♠	church
🛆	tower (observation, water, etc.)
⛴	ferry
⛫	lighthouse
▮	boat ramp

10

Those who would like more detailed maps should obtain U.S. Geological Survey topographic sheets (available at many sporting goods stores). In addition, the Rhode Island Department of Environmental Management prints maps of its management areas, and the Audubon Society of Rhode Island can provide maps of some of its properties.

I hope you will find that this is a book of far more than 40 walks. In order to really know these trails, you should walk them in each season. A woods path is completely different in snow than it is in summer. Why choose between wildflowers in spring and glorious autumn foliage? Enjoy both. Also, if you walk the routes in reverse direction, you will get still another perspective. So instead of 40 walks, you can make hundreds from these trails.

Revising this book for a second edition required walking many miles over mostly familiar paths, but I found myself getting excited about Rhode Island's trails all over again. Many are, in effect, new trails. If you haven't been on these paths before, you are in for a treat. If you are walking them again after not having seen them for a few years, I think you'll cherish the experience. It's like visiting an old friend who has blossomed with maturity.

Wear orange clothing from 2nd Sat. in Oct. through Feb.

1. Great Swamp   70 miles

A walk around a wildlife marsh to see holly trees and ospreys

Hiking distance: 5½ miles
Hiking time: 3–3½ hours

O ne of the primary reasons for choosing one walk over another is the chance to see something different. At the Great Swamp in South Kingstown you'll see several things not normally found elsewhere, particularly the holly trees and the ospreys.

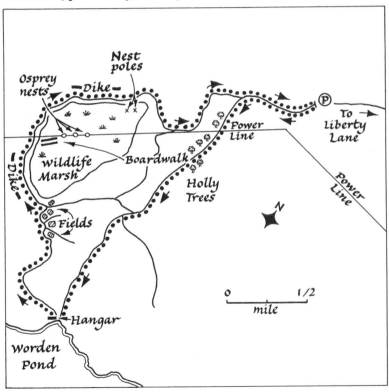

There are not many places more interesting for those who see hiking as more than mere walking. The route described here is an easy 5½-mile loop that runs through a dense woodland, visits a large pond, then wanders by management fields and follows a dike around an intriguing wildlife marsh. For those who so desire, there also is a boardwalk directly across the marsh, nearly under the power-line poles on which the ospreys nest. The entire route could be walked in a couple of hours but usually takes much longer—there are so many reasons for lingering.

The 3,000-acre Great Swamp is one of the state management areas that caters to sportspeople, but in doing so it also contributes immensely to the proliferation of all kinds of wildlife. Once this place was the last stronghold of Rhode Island's American Indians; now it is home to many plants and animals that have been virtually obliterated elsewhere in the state.

The best time to make this walk is early spring, even though the swamp roads are open to walkers all year. In autumn and early winter the area teems with hunters. In summer poison ivy, mosquitoes, black flies, and the heat associated with most swamps can add up to discomfort. In early spring, however, the place is a delight. Be sure to bring binoculars and perhaps a camera with a telephoto lens.

ACCESS

To reach the Great Swamp, take RI 138 to the village of West Kingston, turn west onto Liberty Lane, and follow the road until it ends at a railroad track. Then go left on a gravel lane about 1 mile, pass office and maintenance buildings, and park in a small lot at a barred gateway.

TRAIL

You will walk on access roads throughout this hike. The woods are both damp and dense, in most cases nearly impenetrable. But there is no need to leave the roads; you can see so much from flat, open lanes.

Tall trees shade the road at the start, and the understory of young dogwoods, blackberries, huckleberries, pepperbushes, and blueberries adds colorful variety. In spring you are likely to see violets beside the road; in summer there will be pretty purple flowers called deer grass; and in winter the bright red berries of the black alder practically glow against the stark background. On spring walks you can expect to see and hear catbirds, towhees, orioles, and other songbirds along this route, at least until you reach the wildlife marsh, where waterfowl, ospreys, and swallows take over.

14

In less than ½ mile the road splits. If you want only to see the marsh, you can take the right fork. For this walk, however, keep to the left. You will be returning on the other path.

The feature of the next section of this walk is the holly. These trees, so eagerly sought at Christmastime, are abundant along this road—you can find more here than anywhere else in the state. Look but don't touch—they are protected by state law. They are especially vibrant in winter, when red berries embellish the shiny green foliage; but they also stand out in early spring, before the surrounding trees and bushes open their leaves.

After crossing a clearing cut for the power line, you will return to a drier forest rich with ferns. Without leaving the road, you can find ferns of half a dozen varieties. Mixed in are creeping jenny and prince's pine, two club mosses also protected by law. And guarding the plants are thorny brambles of greenbrier.

You will pass several side trails, but stay on the main gravel lane. When you enter an area dotted with large boulders and low ledges, you will be nearing Worden Pond, a shallow, 1,000-acre pond that forms the southern boundary of the management area. The lane ends beside a federally owned seaplane hangar at the water's edge, but you can take a few minutes to look over the pond, a popular fishing spot.

To the right, as you approach the hangar, you will see a more obscure trail going over a boggy area. When you are ready to leave the

A boardwalk enables visitors to venture out into the Great Swamp.

pond, take this lane. Only the first few yards are wet, and in a short distance the overgrown road opens onto a grassy, pleasant path that winds uphill through the woods. This path leads to numerous small fields planted in grain or left as meadows for the benefit of wildlife. At each field there is a birdhouse erected for bluebirds, but in most cases the residents are tree swallows.

The walking can get a bit tricky here. A general rule is to go left at each fork. You will soon emerge onto a gravel road. Turn left again, heading downhill, and in minutes you will find yourself on the dike, built in the 1950s to create the 140-acre marsh.

This may be the best segment of the walk, especially for those who like birds. Numerous wood-duck houses dot the marsh, and swimming among the lilies and other aquatic plants are usually ducks, swans, and geese. Herons and kingfishers are common, and swallows fill the air (and most of the duck houses).

More likely to capture your attention, however, are the ospreys—the big, fish-eating hawks once close to extinction in New England. To the right you can see the string of power-line poles across the marsh, and balanced atop many of the poles are the osprey's bulky nests. No other place in the state has an osprey population that can rival the Great Swamp's, and the grassy dike offers a superb place to sit and watch these graceful birds.

In early spring, while the ospreys are adding sticks to their nests, you can approach close enough for good photographs on the boardwalk that runs under the lines (if you don't mind wires in your pictures). You may be prohibited from using the boardwalk during the brooding season, however, in order to prevent disturbing the parent birds.

Along the left side of the curving dike is shallow water that features turtles, frogs, and wildflowers. Beyond the stream is a junglelike tangle of dense undergrowth.

Shortly before the end of the dike, in the marsh on your right, you can see two more poles with platforms on top. These were put up expressly for the ospreys, and on my last visit one was in use. You can photograph the action at this nest with a telephoto lens and will have no problems with wires. It's a perfect place to linger before heading back into the woods.

The final segment of the trail swings slightly uphill, passes under the power lines briefly, and rejoins the road you began on. A left turn and short walk takes you back to your car.

2. Trustom Pond

One of the best birding walks through a former farm to a coastal sanctuary

Hiking distance: 3 miles
Hiking time: 1½–2 hours

T rustom Pond is for the birds—and that's the way the people who manage the place want it. On this walk you will see a great variety of birds and will note just how much effort has been put into making this coastal sanctuary appealing to them.

Trustom Pond National Wildlife Refuge encompasses far more than the saltwater pond of its name. The refuge also takes in what once was a farm, and the trails run along open fields, through abandoned pastures now being reclaimed by forest, and past low-lying marshes. You can visit each terrain on this 3-mile walk and, as a bonus, look over a windmill left over from the days when this was a thriving sheep farm belonging to the Alfred Morse family, which eventually donated the property to the U.S. Fish and Wildlife Service. A sheep shed and a small hunters' cabin that were along the trails for several years were recently moved. They now stand near the refuge maintenance building.

Throughout the area there are birdhouses and nesting aids for birds ranging from purple martins to ospreys, from bluebirds to wood ducks. On a good day, perhaps a sunny morning in May, you might find as many as 40 or 50 species of birds on this easy, comfortable ramble.

ACCESS

To reach the refuge, take US 1 in South Kingstown to Moonstone Beach Road. Follow that road 1 mile and turn right on Matunuck Schoolhouse Road. The refuge entrance is 0.7 mile on the left.

TRAIL

A walkway from the parking lot leads to a kiosk that describes the sanctuary and outlines the trails, called the Osprey Point Trail and

17

the Rolling Meadows Trail. You'll travel both paths on the walk described here.

Your birding begins immediately. On a short stroll to the trails' starting points, you will pass through a thicket of bushes where you are likely to find warblers, catbirds, thrashers, and other songbirds. When you emerge into an open field, look for bobolinks, meadowlarks, and perhaps a hunting marsh hawk.

Follow the trail that cuts straight across the open field. This is Osprey Point Trail. You will return by way of Rolling Meadows Trail. Both trails are marked with signs and arrows and are open and easy to follow.

After crossing the open hay field, Osprey Point Trail turns to the right, follows a stone wall, and then goes left through an area filled with bushes and small trees. There are a great many wild berries growing

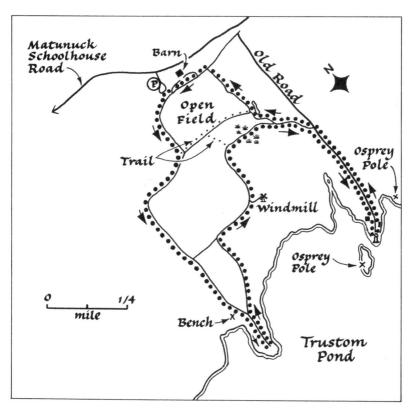

Trustom Pond offers a quiet refuge for waterfowl and contemplative strollers.

here—blueberries, raspberries, wild cherries, viburnums—and, consequently, birds are usually abundant. Robins, catbirds, jays, orioles, and many others congregate here in summer.

Stay on the trail, carpeted much of the way with wood chips, as it passes two cutoff paths to the left. At the second cutoff you will see a wooden bench. You will eventually take this path, but first follow the main lane out onto a point that reaches into Trustom Pond. There are usually terns, geese, ducks, and swans on the pond, and if you look to the left, you can see a small island on which a pole and platform have been erected for ospreys. The platform nest is often in use, and you may want to linger here, watching the graceful fish hawks.

The very tip of the point is an excellent observation point. Across the pond is Moonstone, the barrier beach that is also a bird refuge.

When you are ready to resume walking, go back up the trail to the fork at the bench. The cutoff, now on your right, is narrow and winding. It runs through another thicket of young trees, including some apples, and briefly follows a stone wall before reaching a grassy lane. Take this lane to the right.

You will enter an area used as a sheep pasture shortly before the land became a refuge. The sheep shed once stood just to your right, but now the entire area is quickly reverting to forest.

By following the lane to the point where it turns left, you can see a windmill and stone walls. The windmill is several yards off the trail to the right, in the shadow of tall trees. It no longer pumps water, but the blades still spin in the breeze, adding an idyllic touch to the scene.

Follow the open trail from the windmill, as it runs parallel to the woods, until it forks. Going left would take you back to the hay field you crossed earlier. But go to the right for the walk on Rolling Meadows Trail.

You'll go through a dense, damp thicket (crossing the wettest area on a wooden walkway), then pass a side trail on the left. You will walk this side path later; for now, continue straight ahead to an old road that follows a line of trees and still another stone wall. Turn right on this shady, picturesque road, and follow it out to a second point in Trustom Pond.

This point is lovely indeed, with sea breezes, more birds, and more pond views. The Morses' cabin once stood here, adding another pleasing touch, but it was recently removed because of vandalism. Now only a pump, a tiny shed, and a few relic apple trees remain of the family retreat.

Benches and an observation tower make birding easy and comfort-

Some trails at Trustom Pond wind through dense thickets now thriving on long-abandoned farmland.

able at the point. A second osprey pole stands on the left, and the shallow water to the right of the point is a haven for shorebirds as well as larger waterfowl.

When you return up the old road, take the path (now on your left) that you walked earlier, then take the cutoff to the right just before the damp thicket. This trail curls around a small pond equipped with a pier, an observation deck, wood-duck houses, and a martin house. Whether you see wood ducks or not, you are fairly certain to see turtles and frogs.

Follow the trail beyond the pond as it runs along the hay field and then turns left. You'll pass the refuge maintenance buildings on your right. This lane will take you to the trailhead and the thicket you walked through when you left the kiosk. Chances are, the warblers and catbirds will still be there waiting for you.

3. Vin Gormley Trail

A long stroll through lovely woods and much more

Hiking distance: 8½ miles
Hiking time: 4 hours

This walk has changed some in recent years. For one thing, it was renamed the John Vincent "Vin" Gormley Trail in 1991 for the man who has been maintaining it, almost single-handedly, for many years. At the time of the trail's renaming, Vin Gormley was 80 years

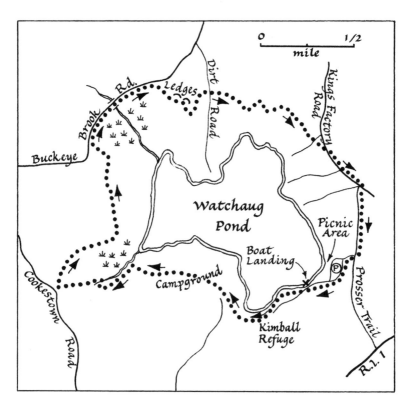

old and still working on the trail two or three days a week.

The trail, running through Burlingame State Park in Charlestown, has been rerouted slightly and now stretches 8½ miles instead of the previous 7¾ miles when it cut across a damp, swampy area. The boardwalk over the swamp was thought of by some visitors as one of the trail's highlights, but the wooden walkway deteriorated and was considered too costly to rebuild and maintain.

The trail's colors have also been changed. Previously, part of it was blazed in white and part in blue. Now the entire trail is bright yellow, and the blazes are often accompanied by yellow arrows.

Most of this walk, though, remains as it was: a delightful and relatively easy walk around the park's Watchaug Pond. The trail still runs mostly through forests with numerous varieties of trees and bushes; it still crosses a busy campground and a quiet bird sanctuary; and it still circles some rugged rock ledges and begins and ends on paved roads.

The blazes are easy to follow, but some care still must be taken because the trail joins and leaves other lanes and paths many times. So don't spend all your time admiring the trees; keep one eye on the yellow marks, particularly the double blazes, which in the Appalachian Mountain Club (AMC) system indicate changes of direction.

Colorful foliage crowds much of the way on the Vin Gormley Trail.

ACCESS

Except for the section that includes paved roads, the entire Vin Gormley Trail is within Burlingame State Park, so the best starting place is the picnic area on the shore of Watchaug Pond. There is not only a large parking area at the pond, but walkers can use the tables for a post-walk lunch and maybe take a swim.

Drive US 1 southbound, west of RI 2 and RI 112, until you reach a paved road called Prosser Trail on the right. Turn and follow Prosser 0.6 mile until you reach the park entrance on the left. You should immediately see the yellow blazes for the Vin Gormley Trail, which follows this entrance into the park and runs along the outer edge of the parking lot.

TRAIL

You can walk either way around the pond, but for this walk begin by going left. The road passes a string of houses and then the park's boat ramp before it enters the Kimball Wildlife Refuge, an Audubon Society sanctuary that is a favorite spot for area birders. Immediately upon entering the refuge, the yellow trail leaves the roadway and breaks off to the right.

In this section the trail runs closer to the 900-acre pond than at any other point in your walk, and you can take side trails to the water's edge. You'll see paths blazed in other colors here too—they are part of the Kimball trail system—so be sure to return to the yellow trail if you wander off.

You will be in the refuge only briefly before breaking into the Burlingame Camping Area, the state's largest public campground. The trail cuts directly through the campground, so you may have to look closely to see the blazes. In summer this is a bustling little city of camp vehicles and tents. You'll walk some paved roads and cross open areas and a couple of traffic islands before leaving the campground on a grassy lane.

You will soon enter dense forest, but the trail remains wide and easy to walk. You'll see a few signs that read "N/S Trail" (for the long-proposed North–South Trail that was supposed to run the length of the state), but be concerned only with the yellow blazes.

Where the trail makes an abrupt left turn you will be making the detour around the swampy area formerly crossed on the walkway. This new section weaves through thick stands of laurel and other bushes, passes stone walls, and crosses brooks on log bridges. It can be muddy in places.

Just as you seem about to emerge onto a gravel road (Cookestown Road), the trail makes a sharp right turn beside a stone wall and remains in forest. This trail leads to one of the walk's most attractive areas, a fine mixture of pines and hardwoods accented with boulders and brooks.

In a short distance you will make a 90-degree turn to the left (the path to the right is the old swamp trail). You will find yourself on an open lane flanked with delightful trees and stone walls. But don't get too comfortable—the next turn (to the right) is easy to miss. If you're wearing a pedometer, this turn is 3½ miles from your start.

For the next mile the trail winds through the forest, again joining and leaving larger lanes before emerging onto a paved road. This is Buckeye Brook Road. Take it to the right. You'll cross a stream and pass a marshy area, but stay on the pavement for only ¼ mile before returning to the woods on the right.

Next you will descend into an inviting beech grove that shades the largest ledges along the trail. The trail runs at the base of the jagged glacial rocks, but you can take side paths to the tops of several of the little cliffs.

Beyond the ledges the trail is very curvy as it gradually climbs away from the unseen pond. You'll cross a gravel road (which runs to a camping area on the pond's north shore) and then enter a hemlock forest laced with brooks and dotted with boulders. After you cross the gravel road, there will be more than 1½ miles of wandering before you emerge from forest again, this time onto a paved road.

Cross the road, returning to forest, and in minutes you will be on another road. This is Kings Factory Road, and your woods walking will be finished. The yellow blazes follow this paved road to the right for about ⅓ mile, then go right at the first intersection. This is Prosser Trail; take it for about ½ mile and you'll be back at the picnic area and your car.

4. Ninigret Beach

A barrier beach walk with a wide variety of ocean birds and seashore plants

Hiking distance: 6½ miles
Hiking time: 2½–3 hours

T he long miles of beach and sand in the Ninigret Conservation Area offer extremes in weather and walking conditions. In summer you have to guard against sunburn; in winter it is a place of icy wind blasts.

But there are many reasons for making this walk, among them the many seashore plants and ocean birds you are likely to see. You will walk the beach to a breachway, then return along the interior sand dunes and the shore of a shallow salt pond.

Ninigret, in Charlestown, is a state-owned barrier beach about 3 miles long. Because it is the first line of defense against storms that

At times, only sea birds accompany walkers at Ninigret Beach.

sweep in from Block Island Sound, it is extremely important to the Southern Rhode Island coastline. It also protects Ninigret Pond, the coastal lagoon known for its crabs, clams, and other aquatic life.

ACCESS

The only road to the conservation area (not to be confused with the more visible, nearby Ninigret National Wildlife Refuge) is East Beach Road. It is reached via US 1, just east of RI 216. If you go in summer, be sure to arrive early. The small parking area fills quickly with swimmers and sunbathers. There is a fee for parking from Memorial Day to Labor Day. In the off-season entry is free.

TRAIL

From the parking lot, cross the ridge of sand to the beach and begin walking east (to your left). In swimming season this first section is likely to be jammed, but proceed to the edge of the water (firm sand is much easier to walk on) and begin. In a matter of minutes you will be beyond the crowds, and after that you will meet only occasional walkers, joggers, and surf fishermen. In the off-season Jeeps, dune buggies, and other recreational vehicles sometimes roar by you, but they are not a major problem.

On a clear day you can see Block Island, which lies about 12 miles offshore. It seems much closer, but distances over water can be deceiving. For instance, as you look east down the beach you can make out the dark line of Charlestown breachway extending into the water. This is your goal. The line is a mass of large rocks and appears to be just a short stroll away. Those rocks are, in fact, 3 miles off.

Still, it is a most pleasant 3 miles. The beach is smooth and clean. The few pebbles at the tide line glisten brightly as each wave washes over them, leaving the small stones polished and pretty. The sea glimmers in the sunshine, and the waves roll in inexorably, breaking white on the sand. On calm days you may find yourself playing tag with the erratic breakers, like sandpipers, as you try to stay dry. On stormier days you may retreat up the beach and watch as the waves pound the sand in relentless fury.

Bring your binoculars because many birds ride the waves a short distance offshore. Look for grebes, loons, mergansers, scoters, and scaups during the colder months. Terns often skim the waves in the summer. During spring and fall migrations numerous canvasbacks, goldeneyes, and other ducks rest here, and at times the beach is alive

27

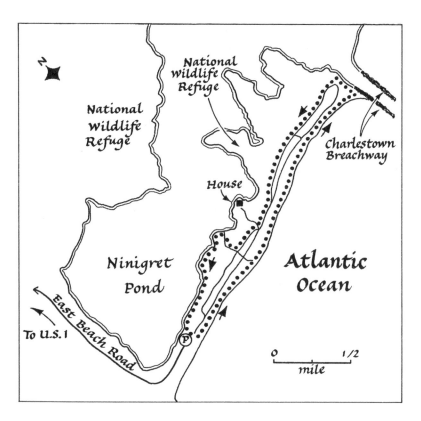

with sandpipers, plovers, and other shorebirds. Gulls, of course, inhabit the beach in all seasons.

On your left, throughout the 3 miles, is the ridge that separates the beach from the pond. Like most barrier beaches it is fragile, and you will see areas where pines have been planted to prevent erosion. There also are many bushes and grasses atop the ridge, along with sections of storm fences that help hold the dunes in place. Walkers are advised not to climb the ridge; even a few crushed plants can escalate erosion.

When you reach the end of the beach, climb the pile of rough-cut stones. It is an ideal place to rest while watching the boats cruise through the channel. On the opposite side there often are people fishing, and you are likely to see campers parked at the western end of Charlestown beach.

To begin the return walk, approximately 3½ miles long and at times more tedious because of soft sand, take the breachway rocks over the ridge. You will be facing north and looking over Ninigret Pond at the abandoned naval air station that is now part of the developing wildlife refuge.

Two sand roads that run the length of the dune end there amid the plants of a salt meadow. Seaside roses thrive in dense thickets, decorating the spot with pinkish purple and white blossoms in early summer and huge orange rosehips in fall. The low-lying, pale-green bushes known as dusty millers are easy to find too, as are bayberries and the vining beach peas. Nearer the water, tall reeds called pampas grass ripple in the breeze.

Egrets, herons, ibises, and a wide variety of sandpipers frequent the pond edges, and you are likely to see swans or geese resting on the calm waters. However, the tangles of bushes and the swampy terrain make walking the pond shore difficult here. Instead, follow one of the sand roads. They run parallel to each other, and the only difference between them is that the one on the right offers slightly better views of the pond.

You will pass through an area designated part of the wildlife refuge, where the roads are lined with wire barriers on both sides. A short time later you will pass a house perched on a knoll on your right, just above the pond.

If you tire of walking in the soft sand, you can take one of the cuts in the ridge and return to the beach. At a well-used cutoff road, however, you can swing to the right and follow the pond the final mile. The walking is easier and more interesting.

You are likely to flush many flocks of sandpipers and will see swallows and other birds swooping over the water. Bits of shells line the shore, and you can expect to see people wading in the shallow pond (average depth is four feet), seeking the abundant quahaugs and littlenecks. You may want to try clamming before reaching the parking lot, and even if you are not interested in clams, the thought of letting that water cool off your feet after 6½ miles in the sand can be almost irresistible.

5. Napatree Point

*Three miles of sand and seabird life, military history, and
a glimpse of what a hurricane can do*

Hiking distance: 3 miles
Hiking time: 2 hours

S ave this walk for autumn or winter, when the swimmers and
sunbathers have gone, the tourists have departed, and the boating
activity around the nearby Watch Hill Yacht Club has diminished.
Then, Napatree Point is an interesting place indeed.

Napatree, a privately owned beach, is as far west as you can go in
Rhode Island and farther south than any other mainland point. It
reaches out into Little Narragansett Bay below Westerly like a slim, J-
shaped finger.

All barrier beaches are fragile, and Napatree is one of the most
fragile. Once it extended much farther into the sea, but the hurricane
of 1938 broke through it. The devastation was immense: Several lives
were lost and practically all the houses and cottages that then lined the
beach were destroyed. Now there are no buildings on the point—only
the remains of a military fort—-and the narrow strip of land is literally
held in place against the forces of the sea by its vegetation. For that
reason, take extra care not to walk on or disturb the plants and bushes
growing down the center of the point.

Napatree Point can be a good place for seeing birds, particularly
migrating hawks in fall, but the birds that nest here require consider-
ation from walkers. As a sign indicates, this is an osprey nesting area
and sometimes there are sections of the beach roped off for the
ground-nesting terns. Because of the birds, it is best to leave your dogs
at home if you visit in summer.

ACCESS

To reach Napatree Point take RI 1A to the village of Avondale, then
follow Watch Hill Road until it reaches a little shopping mall at the
water's edge. You can see the yacht club on the right. Finding a parking

place in summer is difficult, but at other times of the year you should be able to park along the street or in the mall lot.

Walk through the mall parking area and follow a road that runs to the right, past private cabanas, to a fence barrier. There is room at the right end of the wire fence for you to enter the finger of land called Napatree.

TRAIL

You will immediately have a choice. A trail runs along the cove shore at the right and another goes left over the ridge, between snow fences, toward the sea. Take the left path, even though walking in the soft sand is tedious. In a few moments you will be facing the ocean and walking near the water, where the sand is firmer and less tiring.

Follow the beach to the right. This area is crowded in summer, but the entire beach is often deserted in winter, except for a few strollers

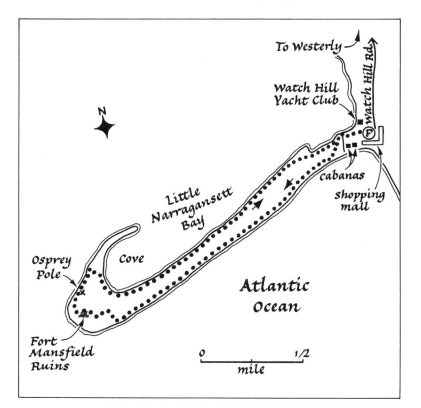

Walkers at Napatree Point are asked to use specified walkways over the fragile dunes.

and an occasional jogger. During September and October you are likely to find a number of birders on the point, for Napatree is a key spot in the migratory flyway of hawks. When conditions are right, hundreds of hawks of half a dozen varieties will pass over the point in a single day.

For more than 1 mile, you can walk a curving shoreline, gulls and other seabirds riding the waves on your left, starfish and bits of shells on the beach at your feet, and the low ridge with its beach plums, dusty millers, and other bushes and grasses on your right. When you finally reach a jumble of large rocks in the water near the point's end, look for a narrow sand path going uphill into a thicket of blackberries, bittersweet, and other bushes on the ridge. Hidden there is something most summertime visitors to Napatree know nothing about—the remains of Fort Mansfield.

The fort was built around 1900 but almost immediately was found to be indefensible and soon was abandoned and eventually dismantled. All that remains now are a few graffiti-marred low walls and concrete steps, a room or two, and the circular holes for the gun turrets, all hidden from shoreline view by the vines and bushes.

From the fort you have a good view of the osprey nests on poles erected at the point. This is also an excellent place to find songbirds that often dally here during migration, as well as a handy spot from which to view the hawk migration.

During nesting season walkers are advised to stay away from the osprey nests—the big, fish-eating hawks once were seriously declining in numbers, and the nest platforms have helped greatly in their comeback. In fall or winter, however, you can go to the shore for a closer look at the poles and nests. Among the rocks at the water's edge you may find sandpipers and other shorebirds, and often there are loons or cormorants just offshore.

From the osprey poles, head for the harbor side of the point for the return walk. Look for a path that will take you across a narrow strip to the smooth cove that lies inside the curl of the J. (Walking the outside shore takes you to a dead end and will add another ½ mile or more to your walk.) The cove is interesting because its shallow, calm water offers refuge for ducks and mergansers and for the many jellyfish that can be seen as you walk along. The footing on the cove shore isn't as smooth as on the sea side—more gravel and mud than sand—but it's still an easy walk back toward Watch Hill.

This can be a very busy place in summer, with boats of all sizes and descriptions coming and going or moored, and boating enthusiasts may want to linger here just as birders often are reluctant to leave the point. By autumn the boating activity declines dramatically; but there are always some crafts moored in the shallow harbor, and the tranquil scene draws many photographers and artists.

The entire walk can be done in a couple of hours. If you like seascapes, migratory birds, boats, and invigorating salt air, however, it could, and should, take much longer.

6. Carolina South

A walk for solitude and a bit of history

Hiking distance: 3 miles
Hiking time: 1½–2 hours

I f you like solitude—a place where you can walk for miles among the trees and brooks and fields without meeting other people—then Carolina South might be ideal. As long as you don't go in hunting season.

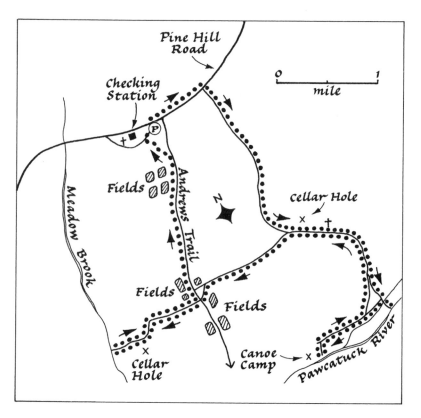

Carolina South is a walk through the southern section of the 1,500-acre Carolina Management Area in Richmond. It is only 3 miles long; but if you want more exercise, it could easily be combined with Carolina North (Walk 7) or you could wander down a few more of the access roads.

The route described here, though short, is likely to keep you interested. You will start near a tiny cemetery, pass another graveyard surrounded by a picket fence and hidden far back in the woods, visit a couple of old cellar holes, take a look at a campsite for canoeists on the Pawcatuck River, pause in a clearing where apple and pear trees continue to survive long after abandonment, and walk along fields planted for the benefit of wildlife.

As with other management areas, this place teems with hunters in the fall, when deer, grouse, and rabbits are sought. For most of the rest of the year, however, Carolina South is left for the walker and an occasional horseback rider.

ACCESS

To reach the starting point from the northern part of the state, take RI 138 east (Exit 3 off I-95) to RI 112 just east of Hope Valley. Go south on RI 112 for 2½ miles to Pine Hill Road, turn west (right), and proceed for 1½ miles. On the left is a red hunter checking station with a parking area in front. If you come from the coastal area, go left on Pine Hill Road just north of the village of Carolina.

TRAIL

First go a few steps from the parking area and look over a tiny cemetery in front of the checking station. Dates on these stones indicate that the last burial was more than 100 years ago. Shading the graves are several apple and pear trees, which add colorful blossoms in spring. It's a pretty, peaceful spot and sets the mood for this walk.

Walk east (back toward RI 112) on Pine Hill Road about 0.3 mile to find the access road on the right where you will enter the forest. A gravel lane at first, the road runs beneath tall pines, and before long the surface is only pine needles and then grass. This road runs along the eastern boundary of the state property, and you will see numerous "Keep Out" and "No Trespassing" signs on your left. As long as you stay on the road, you are okay.

When the lane makes a sweeping curve to the left, following a stone wall, you will enter a clearing now being devoured by the surging

35

woods. Wild grapes and greenbrier vines swarm over the rocks and logs, and saplings of a dozen species compete for growing space. Still holding their own are a few apple and pear trees, which bloom defiantly each spring and produce some small, misshapen fruit late each summer. These trees are proof that this was once a home site; off to the left of the trail you can find a cellar hole, now little more than a pile of tumbled stones.

You'll pass a grassy lane running to the right. For now stay on the main road. Later the grassy lane will be your route to the fields area. Soon you will see the cemetery surrounded by a faded, white picket fence. This graveyard is not as old as the one along Pine Hill Road; some stones are dated after 1900. The fence makes the cemetery unusual; most similar graveyards are guarded by stone walls.

A few yards beyond the cemetery the road forks. Take the left branch downhill and then go left again at the next junction. Here you can cross a brook on a stone bridge and follow a narrow path to the Pawcatuck River. The path also turns left and runs out to an open field, but at that point it leaves state property. So after looking over the river, recross the bridge and take a left on a path that runs parallel to the brook, which soon empties into the river.

Far back in the woods of Carolina South, a picket fence surrounds a family graveyard.

You will quickly pass a lane coming in from the right (your return route), and you will briefly follow a stone wall. Beyond the wall you can see boulders and bedrock ledges back in the woods, one of the few rocky areas on this walk.

Look for a cutoff trail to the left. It runs a short distance to the canoe campsite on the riverbank. The camp is little more than a small clearing for tents and a rock-ringed fireplace, but it offers a good view of the Pawcatuck and a place to linger.

The woods road past the camp cutoff eventually dead-ends at a fence, so retrace your steps east to the lane you passed earlier. Take it north (left), and go uphill until it rejoins your original road just below the cemetery.

When you reach the open lane you passed earlier (now it is on your left), take it. At times it is barred to vehicles, but walking it is permitted. You can follow this lane through a mixed forest to the center of the management grounds.

When the lane emerges at a small field, look for a left fork that runs through another small woodlot to a larger field. Walk the edge of the field to the left, to a gravel road. This is called Andrews Trail on management maps, and it cuts through the heart of the fields area. You can go left here and look over numerous grain and meadow parcels, or turn right and walk back to the checking station.

A third option is to cross the gravel road, walk the edge of a field, and look for a narrow lane that angles to the left into the woods. Just a few yards down this lane, hidden in a tangle of old lilacs and other bushes on the left, is a cellar hole that features a huge foundation of a center chimney.

The trail continues to a rocky crossing over a stream called Meadow Brook. The stream is worth a look, but in order to return to your start, a backtracking to the gravel Andrews Trail is recommended.

After turning north (now left) on Andrews Trail, you will be on the final segment. The road runs between open fields at first, then goes through a forest of mostly pines for some distance before reaching fields again. Go slowly—there may be deer or wild turkeys anywhere along this section. When you can see the checking station ahead to your left, you will be nearing the end of the walk. Your car will be straight ahead.

7. Carolina North

Laurel, hemlocks, songbirds, and grouse, and perhaps a look at wild turkeys

Hiking distance: 4 miles
Hiking time: 2 hours

S ave this walk for some bright morning in May. That's when a stroll through the northern segment of the Carolina Management Area in Richmond is most rewarding, because you will be likely to see numerous birds, possibly including wild turkeys.

Absent from Rhode Island for more than 150 years, wild turkeys have been reestablished through a state stocking program, and the big forests of Carolina are among their favorite habitats. Walking there offers other delights too, but the turkeys make the place unique, especially in spring when the gobblers are noisy.

This 4-mile walk is called Carolina North because it lies on the north side of Pine Hill Road, which slices through the 1,500-acre management area. There is another ramble called Carolina South (Walk 6) on the opposite side of Pine Hill Road.

Carolina North's entire walk is on management roads marked with name posts. You will start on perhaps the most commonly used road, then cut through the heart of the forest, and return on a seldom-used lane that returns you to Pine Hill Road.

The loop can easily be done in 2 hours. As with many management areas, dogs must be leashed if you walk here between April 1 and August 1.

ACCESS

To reach the starting point for both Carolina walks from the northern part of the state, take RI 138 east (Exit 3 off I-95) to RI 112 just east of Hope Valley. Go south on RI 112 for 2½ miles to Pine Hill Road, turn west (right), and proceed for 1½ miles. On the left is a red hunter checking station with ample parking near the road. If you will be coming from the coastal area, go left on Pine Hill Road just north of the hamlet of Carolina.

TRAIL

Walk Pine Hill Road a short distance west from the checking station, cross a stream called Meadow Brook, and take the first gravel lane to the right into the forest. Meadow Brook is a popular trout stream in spring, and this lane, identified by a signpost as Meadowbrook Trail, has several cutoffs to the stream for people who fish. The access roads are busy in fall as well, when hunters scatter through the woods in search of deer, grouse, and rabbits, and snowmobilers use them in winter.

Meadowbrook Trail is shaded by tall pines for the first ½ mile, and in May you are likely to hear numerous songbirds in the dense woods as well as turkeys. There may also be grouse "drumming"—calling potential mates with loud sounds created by beating the air with their wings.

Beyond the first cutoff to the stream, you will pass a gravel lane called Essex Trail that goes to the left. In this area there are several

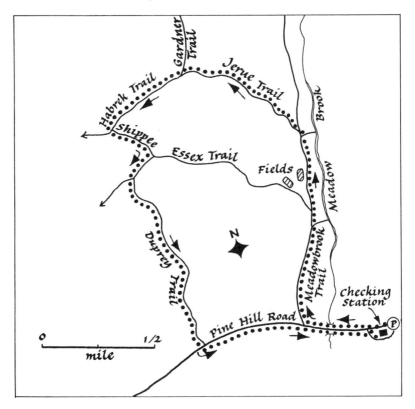

Quiet lanes make walking at Carolina North easy and comfortable.

small clearings and fields designed to attract and feed wildlife. When you reach the second cutoff to the stream (going to your right), there is a fork in the lane. The way to the right is barred. Go left—a signpost identifies this lane as Jerue Trail.

Jerue, which has less traffic than Meadowbrook, winds around much more and is a bit more hilly. The forest is mostly second-growth hardwoods with a great deal of mountain laurel in the understory. Dogwoods bloom in May, and there are numerous wildflowers and ferns along the lane.

You will pass a network of stone walls that indicate that this was once farmland. Look for a venerable old beech tree covered with carvings, mostly initials dating from the 1940s.

Stay on Jerue, passing a lane called Gardner Trail, until you reach a T junction, then turn left. You will be on Habrek Trail. Forest is thick on both sides, with many young trees crowding the trail. You will be walking mostly downhill. If it is May, you'll notice several old apple trees in blossom, an even more vibrant legacy to the vanished farmers than the many stone walls.

At the next lane junction, often barred, take another left. A signpost identifies this lane as Shippee Trail. Going right on Shippee would take you to the Carolina Trout Pond. By going left you will be heading back into the interior of the forest. You'll see more old apple trees and many lovely pines, and you will be walking slightly uphill.

Shippee soon ends at a crossing at Essex Trail. To the left, Essex would take you back to Meadowbrook. Instead, turn right on Essex, then, almost immediately, take a left on a path called Duprey Trail.

You will follow Duprey for almost 1 mile, all the way back to Pine Hill Road. It is a delightful path that is often carpeted with pine needles or grass, both of which are welcome after the miles of gravel lanes. There are attractive hemlocks and impressive thickets of mountain laurel in the section too, as well as areas of open woods dotted with large boulders and divided by stone walls. The laurel may make you want to return in June, when it will be in bloom.

You will emerge onto the paved Pine Hill Road near utility pole No. 71. Turn left, round a bend, and you will quickly reach Meadowbrook Trail (at pole No. 68) where you entered the forest. Your car will be just ahead on the right.

8. Long Pond–Ell Pond

A strenuous walk to three ponds, a "cathedral" in the woods, and a "magnificent mile" of wild rhododendrons and hemlocks

Hiking distance: 4½ miles
Hiking time: 3 hours

This walk is through a forest now called the Long Pond–Ell Pond Natural Area, and outstanding natural features are just what you will find. The first section is so spectacular it might be called the "magnificent mile."

In addition to Long Pond and Ell Pond, you will visit Ashville Pond. A full circuit runs about 4½ miles and will take you 3 hours or more.

The path is the southern terminus of the Appalachian Mountain Club's (AMC's) Narragansett Trail (Walk 9), which also goes into Connecticut. Included on the fairly strenuous walk are climbs up rocky overlooks above the ponds, a descent through a deep gorge, pauses beneath towering rhododendrons and hemlocks, and a look at several unusual rock formations, among them a cathedral-like setting in the woods.

In 1974 this area was entered in the Registry of Natural Landmarks because the site "possesses exceptional value as an illustration of the nation's natural heritage and contributes to a better understanding of man's environment." A plaque with those words is embedded in a boulder above Ell Pond.

ACCESS

To reach the start of this walk, follow RI 138 to the Hopkinton village of Rockville, near the Connecticut line; turn left onto Wincheck Pond Road, then left (south) onto Canonchet Road. Drive ½ mile to North Road and follow it 1 mile. After ½ mile the roadway becomes gravel. Park on the left, where you see a sign and the yellow AMC trail blazes. There is another parking lot ½ mile south on Canonchet Road, but the North Road access is closer to the region's best sights.

TRAIL

Almost immediately you will be scrambling up, down, and around boulders, but you are more apt to be looking above your head than under your feet. Some of the tallest wild rhododendrons in the state shade the trail here, as do hemlocks and mountain laurel. In early summer the profusion of blossoms in the first 200 yards creates a gardenlike atmosphere.

Remember, however, that this is not a walk for those out of shape. By the time you reach the high bluffs above Ell Pond and Long Pond, less than ¼ mile from the start, you are likely to be huffing and puffing, and the climbs get tougher on the far side of the ponds.

After struggling up a huge, angular rock mass, you will reach an intersection. The yellow-blazed trail plunges straight ahead—and straight down—through the gorge. Side paths break off to the left and right, and both are worth exploring before venturing into the gorge.

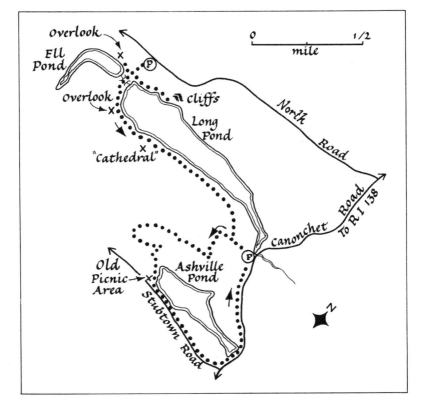

To the right, you will emerge onto a bluff overlooking Ell Pond. The shallow, L-shaped bog, one of Rhode Island's few true bogs, is nearly 70 feet below you. The vista is likely to make you linger.

The cutoff to the left from the main trail winds around to another series of high bluffs, this time facing Long Pond. These rocks were once a gathering place in warmer months for young people who partied here while diving off the lower cliffs into the pond and who left behind beer cans and broken bottles. The bluffs are considerably cleaner now that the area is patrolled by a state ranger. Ownership of the property around the ponds is shared by the state, the Nature Conservancy, and the Audubon Society of Rhode Island.

Back on the yellow trail, ease yourself down into the gorge. It is steep and narrow, but an AMC work force recently rearranged some of the rocks and now the descent is much easier, almost a stairway. Solid walls of stone tower above you on both sides.

You will round a bend at the bottom of the cleft and cross a bridge over a brook that links the two ponds. The trail then curves left along a steep slope, winds through numerous strenuous drops, and rises toward Long Pond. Twice you will emerge onto rocky overlooks that provide excellent views across the water to the high bluffs you visited earlier.

You will also climb through the rocky area I call the "cathedral" and enter through an archway of rhododendrons. The ceiling is dense hemlock, so thick the "room" is permanently dimmed. Huge rocks jumbled across the steep slope represent the pews. Pick your way up the narrow aisles until the trail leaves the hemlocks. As you pass through here, you may find yourself speaking in hushed, reverent tones. I often do.

There is more up-and-down going beyond the cathedral, until you see a tumbledown stone wall. For the next several hundred yards, follow the wall atop a stony ridge, high above the narrow pond. When you finally turn right, away from the pond, you will be near a short side trail to the left that takes you to the Canonchet Road parking lot. The yellow-blazed trail, however, swings abruptly right, then left, for the walk to Ashville Pond.

It is 1 mile from this point to Ashville Pond, though the walking is considerably easier than in the first mile stretch. For much of the way you will walk through thickets of mountain laurel. It is an easier, if less spectacular, segment than the blossomed area around Ell Pond.

The trail ends at picturesque Ashville Pond in an abandoned picnic area, where there are still old outhouses and a shelter. I prefer returning by taking the paved Stubtown Road to the left to Canonchet Road. (To the right, Stubtown ends at a landfill.) When you reach Canonchet, go left again, passing along the other side of Ashville Pond, and continue all the way to the Canonchet parking lot, where the yellow blazes can be picked up once more.

The return walk is slightly longer by road, but it is also faster and you avoid having to retrace your entire hike.

From the Canonchet parking lot, you will have to rewalk the ridges and gorges around Long and Ell ponds to your car, but it is only 1 magnificent mile.

Lichen-covered rocks and dense foliage guard the trails at Long Pond and Ell Pond.

9. Narragansett Trail

A walk through thickets of laurel, over rock ledges and numerous brooks, to a spectacular ravine

Hiking distance: 4 miles
Hiking time: 2 hours

This section of the Narragansett Trail in Hopkinton has changed more than once in recent years, but it continues to provide splendid scenery as well as plenty of exercise. Because of problems involved in crossing private property, I recommend staying on the north side of Yawgoog Pond for this walk and making a separate hike out of the area south of the pond. That section is the Long Pond–Ell Pond Trail (Walk 8).

Nearly all of this 4-mile walk is in Connecticut, although it starts and ends in Rhode Island. It visits a massive outcropping called Dinosaur Rock on the Rhode Island side of the line before it swings across to picturesque Green Falls Pond and its magnificent ravine in Connecticut.

The route also rambles through large thickets of mountain laurel, climbs numerous rock ledges, crosses tumbling brooks, and passes a log shelter before returning on a little-used gravel road. This trail hooks up with Tippecansett South (Walk 10) early in the walk, so you have the option of lengthening the hike by walking part of that trail.

ACCESS

To reach the trailhead, take RI 138 west of Rockville a short distance to Yawgoog Road. Follow the paved road to the entrance of the Yawgoog Scout Camp, then turn onto the gravel road that runs to the right outside the camp. Take the gravel road for 1.2 miles to the state line.

You will begin seeing yellow blazes along the road, but continue driving until the yellow trail goes into the woods on the right. At this point you will also see blue blazes, which indicate Connecticut trails maintained by the Appalachian Mountain Club (AMC). On the left side of the road is a concrete post that designates the state boundary. There is room enough for two or three cars to be parked on the right shoulder.

TRAIL

At the start, as you enter the woods on the right side of the road, you will be following both the yellow and blue blazes because this segment virtually straddles the state line. Immediately, you will pass through the laurel thickets that remain green all year and blossom spectacularly in June.

In less than ½ mile the trail forks, the blue blazes curve left and the yellow blazes go right. For now take the yellow path. It drops through a small ravine, then climbs the huge stone ridge known as Dinosaur Rock. This rock is the southern terminus of the Tippecansett South Trail. By continuing north on the Tippecansett, you could walk all the

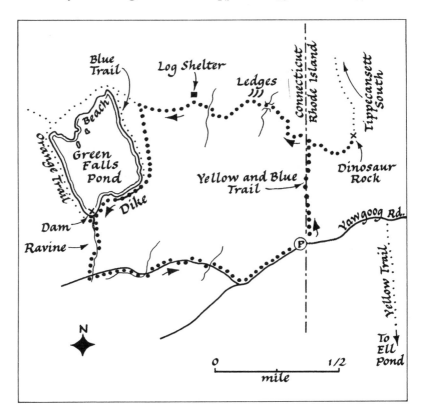

47

A high dam separates Green Falls Pond from the gorge on Narragansett Trail.

way to Beach Pond, and then on to the many trails of the Arcadia Management Area, but for this walk, turn around here after taking time to examine Dinosaur Rock.

When you return to the yellow-blue trail junction, take the blue path into Connecticut. The trail climbs over boulders and ridges and crosses one rushing stream on a single-plank bridge. When you reach the second brook, the trail curves right, following the brook briefly before crossing near the remains of a stone foundation.

Just beyond the stream the trail breaks into a small clearing dominated by a three-sided log shelter used by overnight campers. In a few more minutes the trail reaches a gravel lane.

You will be near Green Falls Pond. The blue blazes go to the right at the lane, swinging down to the water's edge, where the path meets another trail that circles the pond. You have three choices: follow the lane left, take the blue path to the water and then turn left, or circle the pond to the right, passing a beach and picnic area.

By going left on the lane, you will quickly reach an earthen dike built along the lower end of the pond. On the left side is a stone retaining wall, and on the right is a row of bushes at the pond shoreline. The dike offers some good views of the pond, its rocky islands and forested shores.

At the far end of the dike, pick up the blue blazes again, and take the path that follows the shoreline into a grove of hemlocks. You will soon see faded orange blazes with the blue (the orange path circles the entire pond), and the path drops down a slope to a stone and concrete dam. If you look to the right while crossing the dam, you will see a shallow pond lapping placidly at your feet. But if you look to the left, you will see a deep ravine, and water that flows over the spillway or through the dam gates cascades down the rock wall.

The blue trail curls to the left at the far end of the dam and drops into the ravine. It then runs along a brook for the length of the ravine, twice crossing the water. More intriguing than the waterway, however, are the high rock walls that tower above you on both sides. Covered with mosses and lichens, and permanently shaded by dense hemlocks, these walls are green, dark, and impressive.

When you reach a gravel road, the blue blazes turn right. You, however, should turn left. This is the same road on which you parked. The walk back to your car will be about 1 mile, but it's a most pleasant mile of stone walls, brooks, laurel thickets, and hemlock stands. With the road virtually abandoned by cars and trucks, it now is simply another part of a lovely trail.

10. Tippecansett South

A trail through the southern portion of Arcadia Management Area to Dinosaur Rock

Hiking distance: 7¼ miles
Hiking time: 3–3½ hours

A t its northern end, you will walk through imposing pine and hemlock forests. At its southern end, you can enjoy dense laurel and rhododendron thickets. These diverse surroundings are part of the attraction of Tippecansett South, the southern part of the long Tippecansett Trail through the Arcadia Management Area.

This trail links two of Rhode Island's most popular walking places along the western border: the Beach Pond area by way of Hemlock Ledges Trail (Walk 11) and the Yawgoog Pond and Ell Pond region via Narragansett Trail (Walk 9). It also connects the two natural zones divided by RI 138. On this walk you can stroll by a tranquil farm, visit two abandoned cellar holes and a massive stone ridge called Dinosaur Rock, and listen to countless birds.

ACCESS

RI 138 makes a convenient starting place with approximately 60 percent of this 7¼-mile walk on the north side of the highway and 40 percent on the south. The trail crosses the highway in Hopkinton at a curve 5½ miles west of I-95 (Exit 3) and 1½ miles west of Rockville village. Leave your car on the road's shoulder at the left, being careful not to block any driveways. Begin this walk by crossing the road, heading north.

TRAIL

The trail, marked at present in faded yellow, follows a gravel driveway past a sign denoting Noah's Ark Farm and then past a house. The gravel quickly gives way to dirt and grass, but the trail continues along the route of the old road. You will pass two side roads going to the right. You will later return to the second of these old, grassy byways for a loop around the farm, but for now continue straight ahead with the blazes.

The walking is slightly uphill, but the lane is smooth and easy. You will soon reach another fork. This time bear right. Within minutes you will cross a wooden bridge and begin a steeper ascent. The trail becomes more sandy and you will notice more boulders and bedrock in the forest. As you climb a depression appears just left of the lane, and you will soon find yourself on the edge of a deep ravine.

Beyond the bridge, about 1 mile from your start, you will reach a roadway lined with stone walls going to the right. This road is barred and posted, so continue on the sandy road as it swings left.

You will be virtually straddling the state line at this point, sometimes a few feet in Connecticut, sometimes returning to Rhode Island.

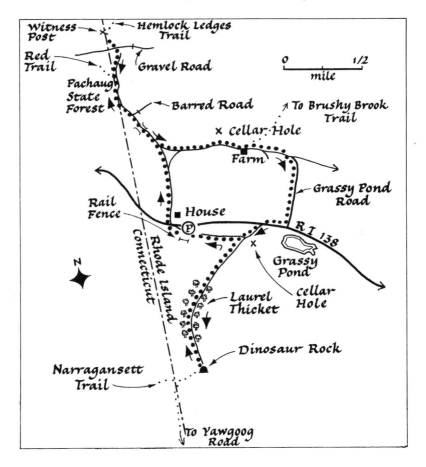

The observant may find a stone marker on the right, with "C" chiseled into one side and "RI" into the other.

On the Connecticut side (left) you will see a stand of tall pines in which some logging recently has been done. On the right, surging undergrowth is reclaiming what once was farmland. This is prime wildlife habitat, and it is not unusual to find deer tracks or grouse dusting wallows on the sandy lane.

Much of the Tippecansett South trail follows serene woodland roads.

At one of the cutover areas you can see a trail blazed in red and blue coming in from the left. This path runs around the Connecticut side of Beach Pond. The yellow trail stays on the lane until you reach a gravel road—the southern terminus of the Hemlocks Ledges segment of the Tippecansett Trail. You can continue to follow the trail into the woods; it emerges onto RI 165 just east of Beach Pond.

For this walk, however, go only a few yards into the woods—until you find the witness post that serves as the state boundary marker—then retrace your route back down the lane, past the barred road and the wooden bridge. In slightly more than 1 mile from the point of your turnaround, you will reach the grassy cutoff trail, now on your left. Take this lane.

At first you will stroll downhill through a dense forest, then climb briefly. When the trail levels off and opens slightly, look for a cellar hole and the remains of a huge stone fireplace and chimney on the left. Behind the house foundation is a hand-dug, stone-lined well covered by a large, rectangular rock. The well is a work of art and is worth examining, but be extremely careful—old wells often are hazardous.

Throughout this section of the walk you will see white blazes. They show that this is the connector between Tippecansett and the Brushy Brook Trail (Walk 37, *More Walks & Rambles in Rhode Island*, Backcountry Publications). Beyond the cellar hole the path runs along one of the overgrown pastures of the farm, following fences and stone walls as it curls gradually to the right. You'll pass another pasture and an orchard, and the white-blazed trail will break off into the woods on the left before you reach the farm buildings. There the lane becomes a gravel road.

For the next mile or so you will follow the roadway, turning right at the first fork. Throughout this section, you will walk between dense forests, and in spring you can listen to a plethora of birds—thrashers, thrushes, orioles, warblers, catbirds, towhees, vireos, and wrens.

When you reach a paved road, you are back on RI 138. A right turn and walk of less than ½ mile would take you back to your car. However, you have not seen the best laurel thickets or Dinosaur Rock yet, so take the highway to the right only as far as the first (unblazed) lane entering the woods on the left. A short walk on this narrow, stone-walled lane returns you to the yellow blazes of Tippecansett, rejoining the trail at a sharp turn beside a cellar hole.

Go left on the marked trail. It is 1 mile through grand thickets of laurel—awesome in early June—to the immense outcropping known as

Dinosaur Rock. Your path will join the Narragansett Trail at this point.

Technically, Tippecansett Trail does not end here—it swings to the right from the rock and ends a short distance farther at the Narragansett Trail. But your car is back on RI 138, so pause a few minutes and look over the smooth ledge. Just why it has been called Dinosaur Rock is unclear, but it is an impressive sight.

Return to your car by rewalking the path through the laurel and turning left beside the cellar hole. You'll pass a house or two along this segment as well as a deteriorating, old-fashioned, zigzagging rail fence. Such fences are now rare in rural Rhode Island, and this one is collapsing in places, but it still represents one more link to the past. It is a fitting conclusion to this walk.

11. Hemlock Ledges

Unique formations of glacial ledges and unusually picturesque hemlocks in this middle section of the Tippecansett Trail

Hiking distance: 3½ miles
Hiking time: 2 hours

H emlock Ledges is the middle segment of the long Tippecansett Trail through the Arcadia Management Area. At one end it links with the Firetower Trail (Walk 12), and at the other end it connects with Tippecansett South (Walk 10). It is short but sweet, adding sights not readily found anywhere else along the Tippecansett.

Both the hemlock trees and the glacial ledges for which this walk is named are unusually picturesque, and in this 3½-mile loop you'll see unique formations, both of trees and rocks. You will go as far as a witness post that marks the Connecticut border before returning to your starting point. It can be walked in less than 2 hours, but there are many interesting places where you may want to linger.

ACCESS

To reach the start at Beach Pond in Exeter, follow RI 165 west about 7 miles from I-95. The pond, which extends over the state line into Connecticut, lies at the bottom of a steep hill. There is a large parking lot on the right beside the pond. There is also room for a few cars on the left side of the road, but state authorities prefer that you use the lot on the right.

TRAIL

Cross the road near the pond to find the trail's start. It is marked with a sign that says "Tippecansett" and is blazed in yellow. This first section runs just back from the shoreline. On summer weekends you are likely to find many fishermen, walkers, and children here, an overflow from the crowded beach.

Because of its heavy use, the area is laced with numerous paths and

55

trails, so be sure to follow the yellow blazes. They will quickly lead you to a higher ridge that curves back toward the shoreline. In a matter of minutes you will be away from the crowds and among the hemlocks and ledges. The path often crosses boulders that offer excellent views of the shallow pond, which, in summer, is decorated with blooming lilies and an abundance of bird life.

Near the end of the pond the trail turns left into a dense hemlock grove and begins climbing. When you reach a fork, 0.7 mile from your start, you will be close to the most impressive ledges in the area. The yellow trail goes downhill to the right, a white-blazed path runs straight ahead, and another white-marked path goes up a steep slope to the left, crossing a rock with the notation "Lookout" in faded yellow paint.

Take the left turn to the lookout first. In a few strides you will be at the base of a high bluff. The path edges to the right and then claws its way up through a crevice. In minutes you will be standing atop the

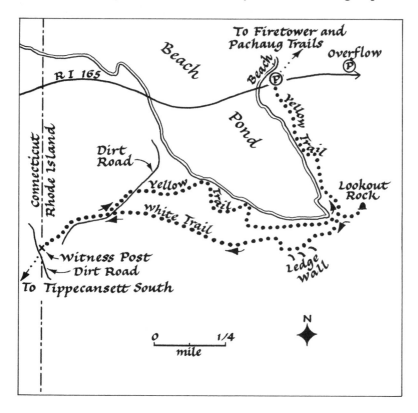

Rocky bluffs and boulders are a featured attraction of the Hemlock Ledges walk.

highest spot in the area. This roundish outcrop enables you to see across Beach Pond to the woods and cottages on the Connecticut side far beyond. For many hikers, this vista is their reason for walking Hemlock Ledges, and they often return to their cars after pausing here.

To continue the loop to the witness post, however, return to the junction and take the unnamed, white-blazed path, now on your left. You will soon reach another white-marked trail with a sign that indicates Deep Pond Trail going off to your left. The word "CONN." and an arrow painted on a tree will keep you on the correct route.

A virtual wall of glacial rock lines the left side of this section for some distance, and you should take your time here, inspecting the trees—most of them hemlocks—that are growing out of cracks and crevices in the ledges. Many are quite old and large, and they protrude from what appears to be solid rock.

The trail continues following the wall until its end, then swings abruptly to the right and curls upward over rocky terrain. You will then walk through an open forest. The hemlocks are fewer in number but more impressive in size, with several magnificent, tall, straight giants. The understory here includes thickets of mountain laurel, which are spectacular when blooming in late spring and green throughout the rest of the year.

When you reach a dirt road, you will be at the end of the white-blazed trail. The yellow trail follows the road here. Turn left, walk a short distance, and watch for the path off the road, to the right, back into the forest of young oaks and blueberry bushes. Within minutes you will reach the metal sign, the witness post mentioned earlier. It stands beside a survey marker embedded in rock: the state boundary.

If you walk a few more feet, you will reach a second dirt road and the northern terminus of the Tippecansett South Trail (Walk 10). For the Hemlock Ledges walk, however, turn around and recross the narrow woodlot back to the first dirt road. Follow the yellow blazes beyond the trail you walked earlier and reenter the woods, farther downhill on your right.

This route takes you through more dense laurel thickets as it winds its way back toward the pond. As you near the water, you will return to hemlock stands and boulders, and both the trees and the rocks increase in size as you gradually climb back toward the crossroads near Lookout Rock. Again, there are many side trails that run to the water's edge. When you reach the junction, go left for the return to your car.

12. Firetower Trail

A car-shuttle walk from Beach Pond to the inspiring Stepstone Falls

Hiking distance: 3¾ miles
Hiking time: 2 hours

This walk is made for an autumn morning. Pick a cool, crisp day when the leaves have turned color, and you are in for a treat.

Firetower Trail runs between two lovely spots: Beach Pond and Stepstone Falls. It is the northern end of the long Tippecansett Trail maintained by the Appalachian Mountain Club (AMC), and it is relatively short, just 3¾ miles. However, because it links with other trails—Hemlock Ledges (Walk 11), Pachaug (Walk 13) at Beach Pond, and Ben Utter (Walk 17) at Stepstone Falls—the ambitious can easily extend the walk if they wish. This is not a walk to hurry through, though; take your time and enjoy the autumn forest.

Do not plan this walk for late November or early December—deer hunting season. A section in the middle of this area is considered prime deer country, and walking there could be very dangerous at that time.

You will be in woods virtually all the way except for a short stretch on two public roads. The first segment is an easy stroll along old woods lanes; then there is a rocky but delightful area, and you end with a downhill ramble through a pine grove and an abandoned picnic area. Along the way you will pass two old cemeteries, numerous stone walls marching through the woods, a spring, a pond, and the fire tower for which this walk is named.

ACCESS

For a one-way walk you will need to park a car at Stepstone Falls. Drive RI 165 west from RI 3 and I-95 about 5 miles to Escoheag Hill Road. Turn right and proceed about 2½ miles to an unmarked dirt road (you will see double yellow blazes on a utility pole at the corner). Go right and follow the winding dirt road downhill until you reach a concrete bridge. There is room to park on the right. The falls are just a few yards downstream.

To reach the trail's start, go back south on Escoheag Hill Road to RI 165, turn right, and drive about 2 miles to Beach Pond, which straddles the state line. You can usually park at the beach and pick up the trail where yellow blazes cross the highway. On the south side of the highway, the Tippecansett Trail is known as the Hemlock Ledges Trail.

TRAIL

For a short distance at the start, the yellow blazes for the Firetower Trail run along with the blue markers for the Pachaug Trail, going uphill from Beach Pond parallel to RI 165, then dropping down a slope. As soon as you cross a dirt road, the paths divide—the narrow Pachaug Trail goes to the left and the Firetower Trail goes to the right on a wider lane.

Go right. It is time to enjoy the scenery. Maples, brilliant in autumn, glow overhead. Birches, beeches, oaks, and ashes add colorful variety.

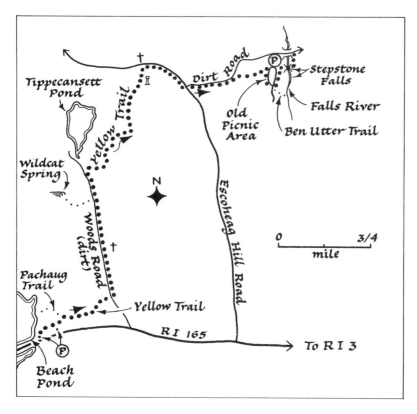

The lane runs gradually uphill but is easy to walk. You will pass some side trails in this segment, but stay with the yellow blazes.

Less than 1 mile from the start, the trail turns left onto an open woods road that is maintained as a fire lane. Stone walls run along both sides of the road in places, and many other walls can be seen in the forest. A short distance along this road you will pass, on your right, a family graveyard guarded by a splendid stone wall and an iron gate. Most of the headstones date from the 1800s.

The next landmark, about ¼ mile beyond the cemetery, is a white-blazed path to the left. This is a pleasant little detour to Wildcat Spring. The winding walk will take you downhill to a tiny spring that bubbles out of the ground beside a jumble of rocks. It runs more freely in April and May than in autumn, but it is worth a look at any time. A visit to the spring and the walk back will add about ⅓ mile to your hike.

Back on the yellow trail, you will soon reach a sharp turn right, marked by double blazes. You are nearly to Tippecansett Pond, but because of the thick foliage the water is often hidden from view.

The path curves around the right side of the pond, and there are spots from which you can see the water but no open, unobstructed views. Some of the area near the pond is private property, so be careful to stay on the trail.

You will cross a small brook on rocks, just below a dam made of rocks; a short time later you will cross an even smaller brook. Immediately after the second brook, the trail makes an abrupt turn left, going uphill. This next section is particularly inviting. Beech trees add a golden glow over rocky terrain. The path snakes its way up over small ledges and ridges. Then, suddenly, you emerge from the woods at the foot of the tall fire tower, which is fenced and locked.

Proceed past the tower to the paved road (Escoheag Hill Road). Take a moment to look over a well-kept cemetery directly across the road, then turn right and follow the pavement around a bend. Watch for the blazes on a pole beside the dirt road on the left. Take the dirt road for the final third of your walk.

You could follow the road all the way to your car, but after about ⅓ mile the yellow blazes turn off into a pine grove on the right. Taking this path will lead you to the abandoned and all-but-forgotten Stepstone Falls Picnic Area, a favorite summertime playground of other generations.

The trail emerges onto a paved road no longer accessible by car, then runs to the right toward a log pavilion. There it meets the Ben Utter Trail.

The fire tower still looms high above the trees on the Firetower Trail.

You will have a choice. You can take a yellow-blazed trail that runs to the left from the pavilion along a well-worn lane. It will take you to your car, just above the river. Or you can go a few yards past the pavilion on the Ben Utter Trail, then turn left onto a white-marked path. This is the one I recommend taking.

The footing on the white trail can be hazardous because it runs over hundreds of rocks, but it will take you to the river, then along the shore to a footbridge just below the shelflike falls. You can cross the wooden bridge and follow a path on the opposite side to the concrete bridge and your car, or you can remain on the near side of the river. Either way, you will be able to finish your hike with great views of Stepstone Falls.

13. Pachaug Trail

A strenuous walk past glacial boulders and sheer cliffs through wild terrain virtually untouched since its formation

Hiking distance: 8 miles
Hiking time: 3½–4 hours

B uild up to this walk. Try some of the shorter and easier trails first. The Pachaug will test your muscles and stamina. It's long—just over 8 miles—and the first 5 miles are among the most strenuous segments in this book. But it's a fun walk and a beautiful one. You climb over rugged ledges in the first part, scrambling up and down ravines and chasms, then finish with a few miles on flat old woods lanes.

This route is actually a combination of three hiking trails and runs a mile or more on an unmarked lane. You start in Rhode Island, swing around a pond into Connecticut, then return to Rhode Island past another pond and a spring.

ACCESS

To start, drive RI 165 about 7 miles west of RI 3 and I-95 to Beach Pond, which straddles the state line. You can park beside the pond unless it's summer and the beach lot is filled. In summer retreat up the hill along RI 165 a short distance to a parking area in what was a picnic area. The Pachaug starts at the beach but runs along the back of the old picnic grounds, so you can start at either place.

TRAIL

The Pachaug is blazed in blue, but you also will see yellow blazes for the long Tippecansett Trail. The paths run together at first, and you will be returning on the Tippecansett, which in this area is often called the Firetower Trail (Walk 12).

Follow the blue and yellow blazes (from the beach or the picnic grove) as they run east, parallel to the highway, for a short distance.

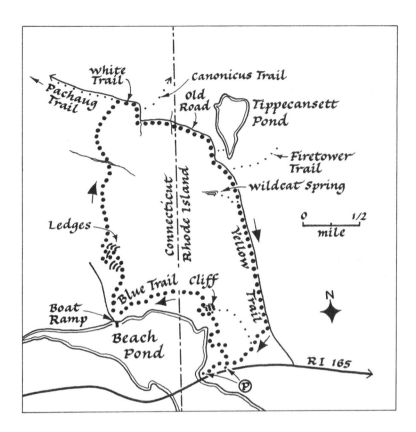

The trails then turn left, drop down a slope, and cross a dirt road before splitting. Stay with the blue trail.

The Pachaug Trail runs back toward Beach Pond, twice going all the way to the shoreline before making a curl around the pond's eastern side. You will quickly get an idea of the terrain, as the trail is rocky and hilly. And it keeps getting rockier and hillier.

If the going appears too difficult, you have an option. About 1 mile from the start, you will reach a cutoff trail, on the right, that runs through the woods to the Firetower Trail. If you stay on the blue trail, you will go west around Beach Pond, soon passing a small blue sign that indicates you are crossing the state line.

Hemlocks and glacial boulders dominate this area and the next few miles. The huge, angular rocks, many of them green with coverings of mosses and lichens, are scattered about, and the trail seems to visit the largest and most picturesque. At times you will walk at the base of sheer cliffs; other times you will pick your way up narrow clefts and around vertical ledges.

This rock-scrambling walk goes on for nearly 1 mile. Gradually you work your way down a slope. When you emerge onto a dirt road, you will be near the pond once more. Cross the road (which is private), and follow the path as it runs to the shoreline, then turns right. In minutes you will be at a public boat ramp.

From the ramp, cross the parking area and pick up the trail again in bushes to the right of the roadway. The path immediately goes back up and over rocky ridges. You will soon cross a dirt lane, and then the trail will level off briefly.

Just as you begin thinking the toughest part is past, the path will suddenly swing left and drop down a deep chasm. At this point you will enter the most strenuous, but also the most impressive, section of the walk. Up and around, over and down, the trail snakes through ravines, climbs ledges, and bounces over boulders. This is wild terrain, virtually untouched since formed by the glaciers. The dense canopy of the hemlocks keeps the ground in permanent shade, and there is little underbrush. Tiny red squirrels are common and birds can be heard overhead, but the area has an eerie, intriguing aura found along few other hikes in this book. It is certainly worth the effort.

Eventually the trail starts to climb and curves gently to the right, finally leaving the hemlocks and entering an area of laurel, hardwoods, and stone walls. You will cross a woods road and then head slightly downhill through a very dense forest.

When you emerge onto the next road, a gravel one, you will have gone about 5 miles. The blue trail turns to the left, but for this walk take the gravel road to the right. You may see faded white blazes, for this is part of Connecticut's Canonicus Trail.

As you round the second bend in the road, you'll see the white blazes and a path break off to the left. Ignore them and stay on the road, which by now is more dirt than gravel. Where the road makes a 90-degree left turn, a lesser lane goes straight ahead. Be sure to turn with the main road—the other lane will lead you astray.

Shortly after the road makes its left turn, you can find cellar holes just off the shoulder, on the left. One old foundation is still shaded by lilacs and surrounded by periwinkles; in spring the flowers are a vibrant, living legacy to the vanished farmers.

In this segment you will cross back into Rhode Island and will soon be walking along the western side of Tippecansett Pond. There are few views of the water, however, and the land on the left is private property. Be patient; up ahead is a spot where you can walk to the pond's edge.

Shortly after passing the cutoff to the water you will leave the pond; then you'll notice the yellow blazes of the Tippecansett (Firetower) Trail. The blazes turn off this road into the brush on the left, but they also run along the road ahead of you. For the remainder of this walk you will follow the yellow blazes back toward Beach Pond.

Moments after rejoining the yellow trail you will pass a white-marked path on the right. This is the route to Wildcat Spring. (See Walk 12 for a description of the spring.) A detour to the spring and back will add about 0.3 mile to your walk.

The yellow blazes will take you along a woods road for more than ½ mile; you will pass a tiny graveyard, then turn right and follow a narrower lane that will eventually take you to the spot where the yellow and blue blazes originally split. From this spot, a left turn and a climb up the slope will take you to the old picnic grove. Beach Pond is just a short distance farther. After this walk a refreshing dip in the cool water may be needed more than a picnic.

14. Escoheag Trail

A gradual descent through state-owned forest to natural and man-made waterfalls

Hiking distance: 3 miles
Hiking time: 2 hours

E scoheag Trail is a pleasant, easy-to-walk path on its own, but it can serve equally well as a warm-up for hikes to a couple of Rhode Island's best wild places. The 3-mile loop described here wanders mostly downhill through a state-owned forest, then returns along an unpaved woods road. At the far end of the loop, the ambitious can easily extend the walk by going up to Penny Hill on the Breakheart Trail (Walk 16) or by following a stream to Stepstone Falls on the Ben Utter Trail (Walk 17).

ACCESS

To reach the start of Escoheag, take RI 165 west about 5½ miles from RI 3, turn right on Escoheag Hill Road, and continue for 1 mile. Turn right on a gravel road next to a log building. This is the old Beach Pond State Recreation Area, now largely unused except by hikers, horseback riders, trail bikers, and, in season, hunters. Turn right again in just a few yards on a narrow lane leading back to a circular drive in what was a picnic area. Park your car here. The white blazes that mark the start of the trail are easy to see at the far end of the loop.

TRAIL

Begin by dropping down a rocky slope, but in minutes you will see a side trail going right, up to the top of a large outcropping. It is worth the time and effort to make the climb, for at the very edge of the ledge is a stone-sided shelter, another leftover from the area's days as a popular place for weekend outings. This spot gave the area its name— the Ledges Picnic Area. It is seldom used for picnics now; but in winter and after the leaves have dropped in fall, it is an excellent place to look over the surrounding woodlands.

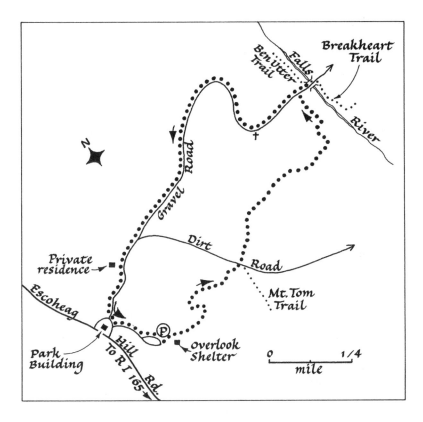

An unmarked trail from the shelter winds around the ledge down to the main hiking trail. Almost immediately you will see that walkers share this path with bikers, and in several spots the bikers have created side paths around wet places, ledges, or other obstacles. Be careful to stay on the white-marked path.

You also will have to look carefully after you skirt the bottom of a large outcropping and climb to the flat top. The trail crosses the table rock and reenters the woods at the extreme left.

This climb is one of the few you will have to make; most of the walk is a gradual downhill stroll. There are numerous little brooks to cross (a great number of them in spring and after heavy rains), but for the most part it is an easy walk. Small beech trees and scattered thickets of laurel make the woods attractive even in late fall and winter.

In less than 1 mile from your start you will emerge onto a dirt road.

Just to your right you will see blazes and a sign for the Mount Tom Trail (Walk 18) coming in from RI 165. Mount Tom walkers either continue on the Escoheag Trail or turn right here and follow the old road back to their cars.

Escoheag Trail continues across the dirt road and runs mostly downhill. The walking is easy at first but gradually returns to rocky terrain similar to the area near your start. There are no ledges to climb, however, and you can proceed quite rapidly and comfortably.

When the trail reaches a grove of pine trees, you will be near the river that is your goal. The path swings abruptly left on an overgrown lane and runs out to a sandy road. This is the road you will walk back, to the left, but first take a few moments to go right to the river.

Just before the river, on the left side of the road, is a sign indicating the start of the Ben Utter Trail, which leads to Stepstone Falls. A walk to the falls and back would add only about 2½ miles to your hike. Across the bridge, on the right, is the start of the Breakheart Trail. If you take it up to Penny Hill and back, following the yellow blazes, you will walk an additional 1¼ miles or so.

Even if you take neither extension, a visit to the rushing stream, called Falls River, is a pleasant diversion. It is a clear, noisy stream that

An old shelter stands beside the Escoheag Trail, a silent reminder of the days when families picnicked in the now abandoned forest.

features natural and man-made waterfalls. They make the place attractive in all seasons.

As you start your return up the road, you may notice a metal sign indicating a historical cemetery in the woods on the left. The graveyard is not easy to find—it's nearly 100 yards back in the forest on a small knoll—but it is interesting. The small, ancient tombstones are weathered and illegible for the most part, but one is accompanied by a rusted metal marker placed by the Society of Sons of the American Revolution. It is a most peaceful final resting place.

The road you return on is barred to automobiles much of the year but is open in hunting season. You are likely, however, to find horseback riders on the road virtually any time of the year. The walk is relatively easy, though the grade is quite steep where the road makes a horseshoe bend to the right. Forest crowds in on both sides and numerous seasonal brooks trickle underneath.

You will pass a dirt road going to the left (the same road you crossed at the end of the Mount Tom Trail) and then a residence on the right. There is another barway here that regulates traffic on the road.

In moments you will be at the old park entrance. A walk down the lane to the left will return you to your car.

15. Frosty Hollow

A winding stroll to Penny Hill through pine forests, over brooks, and through thickets of mountain laurel

Hiking distance: 7 miles
Hiking time: 3 hours

I f you like woods walking, and are in no hurry to get anywhere in particular, Frosty Hollow is your trail. It wanders around in an erratic manner and ends where it began, but it can be a thoroughly enjoyable walk.

Still another hike in the Arcadia Management Area, this route is actually a combination of three established paths. It begins at a trout pond, goes past a small camping area, through a delightful pine forest, across a stream, through an abandoned complex of cabins, then uphill

Abandoned cabins of an old campground suddenly appear in the forest along the Frosty Hollow trail.

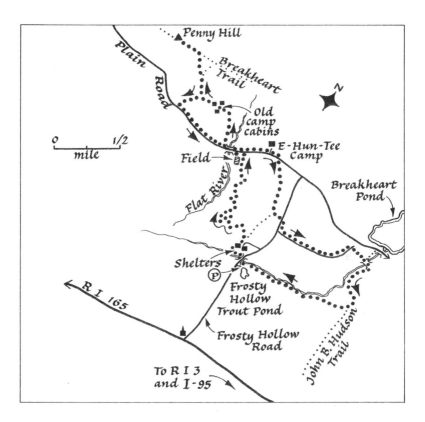

to Penny Hill. That's only the first half of this walk. You then recross the stream, walk along a dirt road, swing through more woods including a parklike segment, follow a picturesque brook in thickets of mountain laurel, and finish up on an easy-to-walk lane.

This route is 7 miles long, but there are several optional cutoffs that would reduce the distance.

ACCESS

To reach the starting point, take RI 165 west from RI 3 about 3 miles to Frosty Hollow Road, then turn right at the West Exeter Church. In less than 1 mile, you will reach Frosty Hollow Trout Pond on your right. Park in the small lot between the pond and a stream, and look for the white blazes at the bridge that crosses the stream.

TRAIL

Officially, most of this route is on a path called the Shelter Trail, but because this route overlaps and uses parts of two other trails—the Breakheart (Walk 16) and the John B. Hudson (Walk 19)—many walkers have taken to using the more lyrical Frosty Hollow name of both the gravel entrance road and the trout pond.

Begin by crossing the road bridge, then follow the white blazes left into the forest. Almost immediately the path swings right and reaches the shelters for which the trail is named. You will pass through the tiny campground quickly, then turn left on a woods lane closed to vehicles. The lane is an easy, open path carpeted in pine needles. In spring you will find violets, lady's slippers, bluets, and buttercups blooming, and you likely will be accompanied by numerous forest birds, particularly thrushes, wrens, and tanagers.

After the lane passes a stone wall and starts curving downhill to the right, look for a sharp cutoff to the left. The trail then becomes quite narrow and wanders back and forth for about 1 mile through a mixed woods dominated by tall pines. Eventually you will find yourself on another old lane that ends at a barway beside an open field.

The trail runs beside a line of pines, past the field to a sandy road known locally as Plain Road. Go left a short distance on the road, cross a bridge, and then turn right into the woods. Once again you will walk on an old lane that narrows to a footpath. After crossing a small brook, the path forks. Go left.

You will climb a rather steep slope and suddenly emerge amid several small cabins, part of the abandoned Beach Pond Camps complex. Once a bustling little village in summer, it is now a place of silence. On a recent visit here I saw a deer stroll through the yard. Take a few minutes to look over the buildings and the rusting water tower, then follow the gravel lane that leads away from the buildings. You can follow the lane out to Plain Road, but the white trail takes a sharp right and reenters the forest.

When the trail splits, take the less-worn left fork. (The right fork goes to Breakheart Trail, and you could then turn right and eventually reach Breakheart Pond.) The left fork runs through a boulder-strewn ravine, then ends at the yellow-marked Breakheart Trail. A left turn and steep climbs up two slopes take you to Penny Hill, one of the highest spots in the area. This is the halfway point in your walk and an ideal place for a rest.

To resume walking, return to the white trail and retrace your route back down to the gravel road at the old camp. Turn right and follow the camp road to Plain Road. A left turn and a walk of about 1 mile on this road will take you beyond the stream and open field you passed earlier. Stay on Plain Road until you reach the entrance to Camp E-Hun-Tee on your left. On your right, a rather overgrown path with faded white blazes goes into the woods. If you can, follow this path to a tree with three small trail signs. One points the way back to the shelters, a second is for the trail you just walked, and a third indicates the route to Breakheart Pond. This is the path you want. In moments you will emerge onto Frosty Hollow Road. (If you are unable to find the cutoff across from E-Hun-Tee, simply stay on Plain Road to Frosty Hollow Road, turn right, and walk until you reach a barred lane called Stone Trail on your left.)

You could walk Frosty Hollow Road back to your car—it's less than ½ mile—but then you would miss some of this hike's highlights. So cross the road and follow the white blazes into the woods along Stone Trail.

The lane runs through a stand of tall pines and curves left before reaching a small parking area for hunters coming in from Plain Road. The path goes along the right side of the parking lot, then turns right and goes a few yards through woods to a former picnic area near Breakheart Brook.

You can turn left and follow the brook to the pond and its distinctive fish ladder; or you can stay to the right, cross the brook on a footbridge, and walk the path that is the return route on my version of the John B. Hudson Trail. The trail turns right after crossing the brook and runs through a glorious thicket of mountain laurel. Follow the gurgling, rocky brook for some distance, then climb to the left to higher ground.

At an intersection of trails look for a Shelter Trail sign nailed to a tree. Take this path to the right and enjoy the final section of your walk. It will gradually descend toward the brook once more, then go through a lovely area of laurel and pines. The trail will take you into the parking lot where your car awaits.

16. Breakheart Trail

A combination of easy and strenuous walking from Breakheart Pond to Penny Hill and back

Hiking distance: 6½ miles
Hiking time: 3½–4 hours

B reakheart Pond and Penny Hill are picturesque places popular with outdoorsmen, but they are remote and nearly unknown to most Rhode Islanders. This 6½-mile walk visits both places, combining an easy walk around the pond with a more strenuous hike through dense forest up to the hill's summit. The walk ends with a 2-mile-plus stroll along a little-used gravel road. Don't let the idea of walking on a road dissuade you—many times walks along roads like this are very rewarding, particularly if you like wildlife. You will see more birds and mammals along rural roads than in dense forests, where the foliage is too thick and the walking too noisy.

This is another walk in the state-owned Arcadia Management Area in Exeter and West Greenwich. The yellow-blazed trail connects with the John B. Hudson Trail (Walk 19) at one end and the Ben Utter (Walk 17) and Escoheag (Walk 14) trails at the other.

A number of the problems of a few years ago have been remedied. Two rickety bridges over brooks far back in the forest have been replaced, and some, but not all, of the erosion problems on steep slopes have been repaired.

Keep in mind that this is a heavily used area in certain seasons, and you may run into fishermen, hunters, horseback riders, motorcyclists, or, as I did once, a dogsled team. There are also numerous dirt roads and lanes and pathways crisscrossing these woods, so be careful to stay with the yellow blazes. Wandering off on side trails could get you lost.

ACCESS

To reach Breakheart Pond, take RI 165 exactly 3 miles west of RI 3. Turn right (north) at the West Exeter Baptist Church on gravel

Frosty Hollow Road, continue 1½ miles to its end, then go right on another gravel road until it ends at the pond.

TRAIL

Before starting your walk, look over the dam and concrete fish ladder beside the parking area. The fish ladder, a series of shallow, rectangular pools, was built to help trout get over the dam and return upstream to spawn. It is one of the few ladders of its kind in the state. Breakheart Pond, as well as Breakheart Brook and Breakheart Road, derive their names from nearby Breakheart Hill, which was named for the heartbreaking task of attempting to drive oxen up its slopes long ago.

To follow Breakheart Trail, swing around the right side of the pond on an open, abandoned roadway. It quickly passes a cellar hole and there are numerous stone walls, showing that this was once farmland.

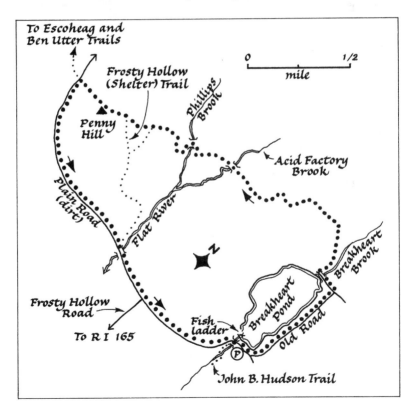

Most walkers of the Breakheart Trail examine an old concrete fish ladder at Breakheart Pond before beginning their hike.

At the far end of the pond you'll reach another old road. You could take it completely around the pond, making an easy $1^1/_2$-mile walk. The yellow trail, however, turns right into the forest immediately after crossing a footbridge over Breakheart Brook.

The trail soon leaves the brook and angles uphill through dense, brushy woods. There are plenty of rocks, but the footing is not difficult. As the ascent grows steeper, the path opens somewhat. Pines and oaks are the dominant trees, and the number of squirrels and chipmunks in the area increases accordingly. On one walk here my young son counted 22 chipmunks and 12 squirrels.

You'll begin crossing unmarked lanes and gravel roads. Be sure to remain with the yellow blazes. Occasionally you will see signs on the right marking the boundary of the University of Rhode Island's agricultural and biological research area, called the W. Alton Jones Campus. No trespassing is allowed.

The trickiest spot of this walk is just after the trail crosses a stream called Acid Factory Brook. The trail appears to go straight ahead, up a slope, but a lesser path that goes left *immediately* after the stream is the one you want. This is the yellow trail; the other is a motorcycle path.

After some minor up-and-down going, the trail levels off through a parklike grove of tall pines, then swings left (again, be careful—cycle paths go straight ahead here too). You'll cross a bridge over a second stream before heading into the most hilly section of this walk.

You will pass a white-marked cutoff trail with a sign that indicates Shelter Trail (see Frosty Hollow Trail, Walk 15) at about the point where logs and stones have been installed in the trail to prevent erosion. In a few places the trail also has been slightly rerouted to avoid muddy areas. As you climb a steep slope, you'll pass a second Shelter Trail crossing and then begin the final ascent to Penny Hill.

The rocky summit of Penny Hill is 519 feet above sea level, and makes you feel you are much higher than the surrounding countryside. The overlooks are about 3.7 miles from your start and are excellent places to pause and rest.

Going down the opposite side is easy, and in a few minutes you will emerge onto a gravel road—Plain Road. Turn left. It is just over 2 miles back to your car, but it is a very pleasant 2 miles with good footing and plenty of birds—and maybe deer—to see along the way.

There are some side roads going off Plain Road, but stay on the main road. It gently curves left, crosses a river, and passes Camp E-Hun-Tee, a private youth wilderness camp back in the woods on the left. There are no other buildings along the entire 2 miles. Once you pass the camp signs, it will be less than ½ mile to the finish.

17. Ben Utter Trail

A leisurely walk along a scenic river culminating at Stepstone Falls

Hiking distance: 3½ miles
Hiking time: 2 hours

The Ben Utter Trail is perfect for those who regard hiking as a relaxing pastime and a means of viewing the handiwork of both nature and humans rather than an athletic endurance event. This trail,

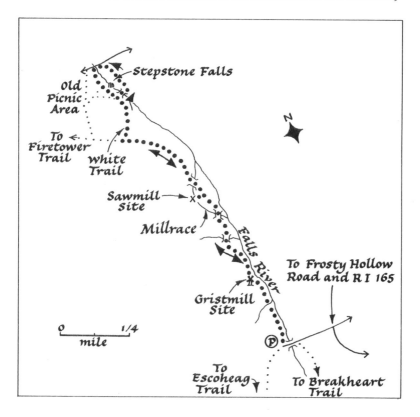

named for one of the guiding lights behind the Rhode Island trails system, is short (about 3½ miles round-trip), relatively level, and very accommodating. Wooden bridges span the brooks, and stone steps ease your way up and down the steeper ridges.

Following the aptly named Falls River upstream, this trail passes the remains of an old gristmill and a sawmill, leads through thickets of mountain laurel and dense growths of ferns, and culminates at Stepstone Falls, one of Rhode Island's most beautiful spots. The trail runs between two dirt roads in the Exeter portion of the Arcadia Management Area and links with the Firetower Trail (Walk 12), the Escoheag Trail (Walk 14), and the Breakheart Trail (Walk 16). This area was once very popular, but the closing of some forest roads in recent years has made access to Stepstone Falls and a nearby picnic area difficult. This trail is now used far less than in the past.

ACCESS

To reach the start, take RI 165 west from RI 3 about 3 miles to Frosty Hollow Road. Look for the white West Exeter Baptist Church at the corner. Turn right on the gravel road and drive to its end at a T intersection. Turn left and drive about 2¼ miles until you cross a river. Park just beyond the bridge, on the right, where you will see a sign for the Utter Trail.

TRAIL

The yellow-blazed trail runs to the right along the river. You will immediately hear and see the first falls, although in this section they are man-made structures—huge logs anchored at each end with rocks—installed years ago to make the stream more attractive to trout. The tumbling waters rumble constantly, adding a pleasing, soothing overtone to your walk.

The trail climbs a stone stairway over the first ridge, once part of an earthen dam built for a gristmill. Some of the mill's stone foundations lie just off the trail on the left, but more remains can be seen on the opposite side of the stream.

You will momentarily break onto an old road, now used mostly by horseback riders, then turn almost immediately to the right into a laurel thicket. In early June it is glorious enough right here, amid the bouquets of pink and white blossoms, to make the walk worthwhile.

Beyond the laurel you will cross a wooden bridge over a rushing little brook that was dug as a millrace for a vertical sawmill powered by a waterwheel. In a few minutes, on your left, you can see what remains of the mill, a rubble of huge stone slabs. Many of these slabs have fallen into the water, but it is not difficult to picture the effort that went into building the mill and digging the channel through the stony ground. Another few yards takes you to a second bridge over the millrace, and off to your right you can see part of the dam that was built in the river to divert water to the mill.

Some man-made falls greet visitors to the Ben Utter Trail as they make their way to Stepstone Falls.

Up to this point you will be continually within earshot of the water, and the moods of the hurrying little river can make each walk here seem different. I've seen the river roaring over the falls in a frothy fury, and I've seen it gurgling over in a gentle lullaby. It all depends on the season, the water level, and the rainfall of previous days. Angry or serene, the many falls offer plenty of excuses for pauses.

Eventually the path starts making a distinct climb to the left, away from the water. But just as you feel you're finally leaving the river behind, you will reach a white-blazed spur trail breaking off to the right. Take this trail. If you remain on the yellow trail, you will go into an old picnic area, now all but forgotten, and hook up with the Firetower Trail. At the old pavilion, however, there is another yellow trail that goes to the right, leading back toward the river above Stepstone Falls.

It's best to take the white cutoff trail. It goes over rocky terrain, but in less than ½ mile you will reach the most impressive falls yet. These are natural; there was no need to "improve" upon what already existed. The river sweeps over the wide, flat rocks as if gliding from shelf to shelf or step to step—hence the name Stepstone Falls.

A wooden footbridge, now a bit rickety, spans the river just below the finest set of falls. The white-marked trail crosses the bridge, goes left a few hundred feet on the opposite shore to an auto bridge, and returns to the footbridge, so you can easily walk all the way around Stepstone. After you complete the circle, you can retrace your steps along the white trail uphill, or take one of the unmarked paths that lead up toward the old picnic area. All of them connect at some point with the yellow trail that runs to the log pavilion. Just beyond the pavilion you can pick up your original yellow trail. Turn left for the walk back to your car.

18. Mount Tom Trail

A roundabout route to Mount Tom, past the ruins of a gristmill, over rocky cliffs, and through a reforestation project

Hiking distance: 6½ miles
Hiking time: 3½ hours

This wandering, roundabout route to Mount Tom in Exeter features a wide variety of attractions. Along the way you will cross rushing brooks and pause atop rocky cliffs; you will inspect the remains of an old gristmill and stroll through a thriving reforestation project.

As a bonus you can shorten your walk without retracing your steps by turning and walking a roadway back to your car. Walk this entire 6½-mile route, however, and you will avoid the paved road, except for the few steps it takes to cross the highway twice and a few more to use a bridge. You will be returning along a quiet, seldom-used dirt road.

ACCESS

Mount Tom Trail, another of the many Appalachian Mountain Club (AMC) paths in the Arcadia Management Area, begins along RI 165 at a spot known as Appie Crossing, about 2½ miles west of RI 3. This is the end of the Arcadia Trail (Walk 20) and virtually across the highway from the beginning of the John B. Hudson Trail (Walk 19). There is little parking space at Appie Crossing, however, and returning there would mean a walk along the heavily used RI 165 or retracing your route, so I recommend driving a few hundred yards farther west and parking near the West Exeter Baptist Church at the corner of Frosty Hollow Road. Look for a barred lane coming out of the forest near the front of the church; this will be your return route. Please do not park in the church lot itself, particularly if you arrive on a Sunday morning.

TRAIL

To start your walk, cross RI 165 and go 0.2 mile down a gravel road called Summit Road, directly opposite Frosty Hollow Road.

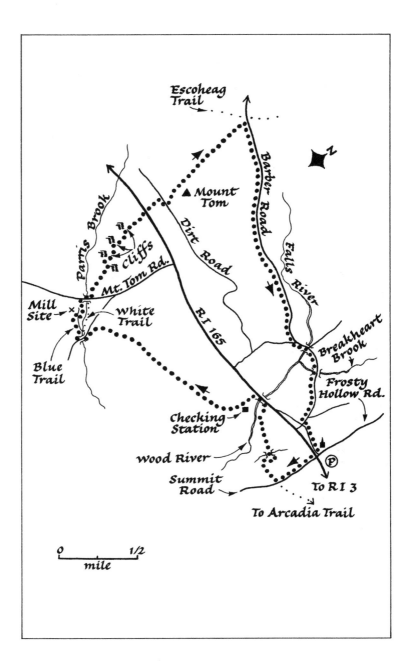

Ignore the first path into the woods (it is a motorcycle trail) and, instead, take the white-blazed hiking trail that crosses Summit Road. Take this path to the right. (You could just as easily start by walking the dirt road in front of the church, but given a choice, I prefer using roads at the end of my walks, when I start feeling weary.)

Once in the woods, go downhill at first, climb a hill, then swing around through a low area and cross a small brook. You will be walking through part of an area replanted years ago after 7,500 acres of timberland were destroyed in one of the worst forest fires in Rhode Island history. Thousands of pines now thrive throughout this region, and all the scars from that tragic fire have vanished.

In less than 1 mile you will reach the Wood River, a popular trout stream. Gravel lanes run along both shores for those who are interested in fishing. It would be shorter to wade through the stream and pick up the trail on the other side, but the blazes lead you to the right over the RI 165 bridge and then back left on another lane, past a Quonset hut that is used as a checking station in hunting season.

Keep an eye on the blazes. The trail uses several access roads, but all are wide, level, and easy to walk. Springtime here is delightful because the pines are alive with migrating songbirds. Young rabbits often lope down the lanes, more inquisitive than afraid, and you are likely to find deer tracks in the sandy soil. In fall and early winter you are apt to meet hunters here, seeking deer, rabbits, pheasants, quail, and grouse, but in other seasons you may have this area to yourself.

Watch the blazes carefully—there are several side roads. The trail leaves the pine grove when you reach a gravel road. Follow the road left a short distance to a stream. The white-blazed trail turns right just before the bridge and follows the stream, but it is better to cross the bridge and follow a blue-marked alternate path on the opposite shore. The blue trail is not as open, but it allows you to visit the old mill site.

The stream is called Parris Brook, and the blue trail soon swings left to follow a separate channel. This is a millrace that leads back to the stone foundation of a gristmill built before 1800 and abandoned now far longer than it was used. Water diverted from the stream continues to run through the mill's immense stoneworks, but the wheel it turned has long since vanished. Still, it is one of the more impressive of the many abandoned mill sites along Rhode Island trails. It invites inspection.

The trail returns on the opposite side of the millrace back to Parris Brook, which rumbles constantly as it cascades down man-made trout falls. Follow the brook left until you reach a paved road—Mount Tom

Road. Turn right, cross the bridge, and bear left into the woods.

At this point you will start the climb toward the cliffs. A lane once ran up this part of the slope, but now brush has virtually obliterated it. Still, if you look closely, you can find some stone embankments and walls that reveal the original route.

Within minutes you will be straddling a ridge. Cutoff paths on both sides lead to rock ledges. The higher you climb, the more ledges you find and the better the views. Atop one overlook, facing east, you

Stonework of a vanished mill provides a pleasant detour along the Mount Tom Trail.

can see for miles, and the scenery is all trees. You may find it hard to believe this is tame, densely populated Rhode Island—it looks for all the world like Vermont or New Hampshire.

Other outcroppings farther on face south and west and they also look over forested valleys. Pines and oaks dominate, but in spring an occasional dogwood in flower adds a dash of color.

The trail along the ridge is all rock. The adventurous and nimble can take shortcuts up and over the boulders. The less agile should follow the trail around the huge rocks. Both routes wind up at the same places—at the end of ledges that drop straight off. It would be a long fall, so watch your step. At the bottom of the cliffs rest great slabs of stone chopped off by the glaciers. They remind me of immense slices of gray cheese whacked off some giant wedge.

More up-and-down scrambling is ahead but fewer cliffs, and shortly, you will descend to RI 165 once more. You will have walked almost 3½ miles, and you can return to your car by simply turning right and following the highway.

But Mount Tom itself still looms ahead. The trail crosses the highway and immediately starts upward. There are fewer rocks, no cliffs, and no open vistas on this part of the trail. For the most part it is an easy but uneventful hike up and over the crest, which at 460 feet is one of the highest spots in the area.

Unlike most hills, it is difficult to tell when you are at the summit. After the initial climb, the trail runs straight and relatively level for its last mile. Bushes and saplings crowd in on both sides, and in places the trail is deeply rutted from trail bike use.

The trail ends on the dirt lane once called Barber Road. Just to the left, the Escoheag Trail (Walk 14) crosses the road. To return to your car, however, turn right and follow the old road. Closed to cars and trucks except during hunting and fishing seasons, the road runs downhill about 2 miles, passing plenty of forest scenes and game management fields and crossing two streams that merge shortly below here to form the Wood River. In spring this is a delightful walk with a great deal of bird activity.

After crossing the first bridge, bear right. After crossing the second bridge, begin looking for lanes coming in from the left. Take the *second* lane (you'll find it where Barber Road seems to split). This lane leads to the church and your car. If you are unsure which lane to take, you can follow the main road out to RI 165. Your car will be 0.3 mile to the left.

19. John B. Hudson Trail

A panoramic view, a stroll through pine groves, a view of a fish ladder, a wealth of songbirds—a good introductory hike for children

Hiking distance: 3 miles
Hiking time: 1½–2 hours

The John B. Hudson Trail, named for one of Rhode Island's hiking pioneers, is one of the oldest in the state trail system, and one of the shortest, yet it remains one of the most popular. It should be—it's a gem.

It is less than 1½ miles long, running from RI 165 to Breakheart Pond in the Arcadia Management Area in Exeter, but sections of it are downright dazzling, particularly in late spring when the thickets of mountain laurel are in bloom and in winter when the gurgling stream it crosses is as pretty as any picture with ice and snow. The trail also offers a view from an observation tower, a stroll through surging pine groves, a look at a tiny cemetery and the cellar of a long-vanished house, and, at Breakheart Pond, a concrete fish ladder. All in all, it packs a lot of highlights into a round-trip of slightly more than 3 miles.

Part of the region's vast Yellow-Dot trail system maintained by the Appalachian Mountain Club (AMC), the Hudson begins almost directly across RI 165 from the end of the Arcadia Trail (Walk 20). At Breakheart Pond it links with the Breakheart Trail (Walk 16). And along the way it crosses the newer, white-blazed Frosty Hollow trail (Walk 15), so extending this walk on other paths is easy.

The "official" Hudson trail has been changed somewhat in recent years, curving away from the picturesque Breakheart Brook; but because the stream is so lovely, I prefer looping back along the old trail. I also suggest returning on a woods road, which not only avoids retracing your steps but adds a pleasant area that includes the cellar hole.

This walk is a good one for giving small children a taste of hiking. Most of it is flat and easy, although the middle segment will involve some scrambling up and down steep slopes along the stream. That area is often muddy and the footing can be treacherous, particularly in early spring, so it might be best to wait until late May or June. Fortunately, that's when the laurel is in bloom.

ACCESS

To reach the start, take RI 165 2.6 miles west from RI 3. Check your odometer because the entrance lane, although marked by a small sign on a tree, is easily missed. The narrow, angling lane takes you to a parking area, on the right, that is veiled from the road by trees.

TRAIL

At the trailhead is a large wooden sign that not only maps this walk but all other AMC trails in the area. The yellow-blazed path first cuts through surging pines, but in minutes you will enter a small clearing. A sign points left to the tower, which you could climb now, but the return route goes directly by the tower, so save that experience for later, as a climax to your walk.

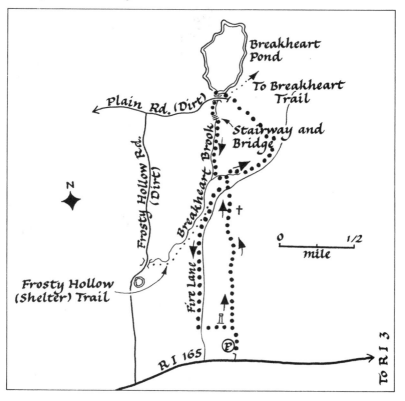

A footbridge spans picturesque Breakheart Brook, a special attraction.

Instead, follow the yellow trail. Almost immediately you will enter the laurel thickets that continue to grow larger and seemingly more magnificent each year. You will be in and out of laurel throughout this walk, and when the timing is right, this can be a stroll through a virtual tunnel of flowers.

The little family graveyard, guarded by stone walls, is just to the right of the trail in a grove of tall pines. The few legible dates range from the 1830s to the 1850s. There among the pines it is a truly peaceful final resting place.

Just beyond the cemetery the trail crosses a woods road called Tripp Trail, which you will walk in two directions later. For now take the yellow trail across the road, noting the signs and white blazes for a path labeled the Shelter Trail (part of the loop I've called Frosty

91

Hollow trail in this book). The yellow trail quickly turns right and emerges onto the wider woods road. It stays on the road only briefly, however, before cutting back into the pines and curving downhill to Breakheart Pond, leaving the forest at a parking area. A bridge and the fish ladder will be just to your left. (See Walk 16 for a description of the ladder and Breakheart Pond.)

To return, cross the bridge and take a path to the left along the stream. In minutes you will reach a footbridge in what once was a picnic area. Cross the stream again, and climb the wooden stairway built into the steep slope. At the top of the stairs turn right. You will be on a white-marked trail that alternately hugs the shoreline and climbs above it. This is the section that often is muddy and slippery, but the stream makes the effort worthwhile. Cascading over thousands of rocks and fringed with laurel and other plants, this brook is as lovely as any in the state.

After some distance the trail makes an abrupt left at a smaller brook and climbs the hill. It then angles to the right until it reaches a junction with the yellow trail you walked earlier. You could now simply rewalk the yellow path back to your car, but I recommend going on it only to the open woods road—Tripp Trail—just a few steps from the white-yellow junction. Take the open road to the right.

This lane, kept open as a fire road, is easy to walk and delightful to look at, flanked by tumbling stone walls and overhanging trees. You will quickly see another road coming in from the right (that one goes out to Frosty Hollow Road), and in the corner where the fire lanes meet is the cellar hole. It is hidden in a tangle of forsythia bushes that continue blooming each spring.

Stay on the woods road until you see a tree on the left with double white blazes. Look for a path, going left, just *before* you reach the tree. This path will take you uphill, and in minutes you will be standing beside the observation tower. (If you happen to miss the cutoff to the tower, you can stay on Tripp Trail to its end at RI 165. Then turn left to reach your car.)

The tower no longer offers the grand views of years past because the surrounding trees have grown so tall, but it is still worth a climb. In winter and before the trees are fully leafed in spring, you can see for several miles.

It's only a few yards back to the yellow trail from the tower. A right turn will take you to your car.

20. Arcadia Trail

A glance back at the past and a look at the future

Hiking distance: 8 miles

Hiking time: 3½–4 hours

The Arcadia Trail in Exeter has been rerouted so much in recent years it qualifies as a "new" place to walk. Now it is about 8 miles long, twice its former length, and ventures into several areas that were not previously included.

The Arcadia Trail still features some of the attractions that long made this a favorite walk—impressive stands of beech trees, rocky streams, stone walls, quiet woods lanes—and now adds stone cairns, a mysterious chimney, great boulder fields, pine groves, and a beaver pond, complete with a lodge and the conical stumps left behind when the beavers cut trees.

Unfortunately, the trail no longer goes through Browning Mill Pond picnic area, a lovely spot in all seasons, but side trails run there. Browning Mill Pond is about the halfway point in the hike, so a car could be left there and the trail divided into two walks.

As before, the trail ends at RI 165 near the start of both the Mount Tom (Walk 18) and John B. Hudson (Walk 19) trails, so the ambitious can easily walk to their hearts' content.

ACCESS

As with other trails in the Arcadia Management Area, take RI 165 (Ten Rod Road) west from RI 3. If you plan to walk the full 8 miles, you will need to leave a car at a small parking lot on the left side of RI 165 2½ miles from RI 3. (The parking lot for the John B. Hudson Trail is almost directly across the road.) Then return 1 mile east to Arcadia Road and turn right (south). You'll pass the Browning Mill Pond Recreation Area and can leave a car there if you wish to do the walk in halves.

To reach the official trailhead, follow Arcadia Road as it curves right and ends in the tiny village of Arcadia. Turn left on Summit Road and drive another ½ mile to the state's Department of Environmental Management complex. You can park in the visitors' lot in front of the buildings. The yellow-blazed trail begins directly across the road.

TRAIL

Begin by walking through a grove of thriving young pines. You'll also see the first of numerous stone walls along this route. In less than 1 mile you will reach and then cross a paved road—K. G. Ranch Road.

Shortly after reentering woods the trail curves left. At the curve you can see, off to the right, granite slabs cut to hold something, probably a granary. The woods here are more open than the first section, with fewer young pines and more wet areas.

Just after crossing a wooden footbridge and immediately after

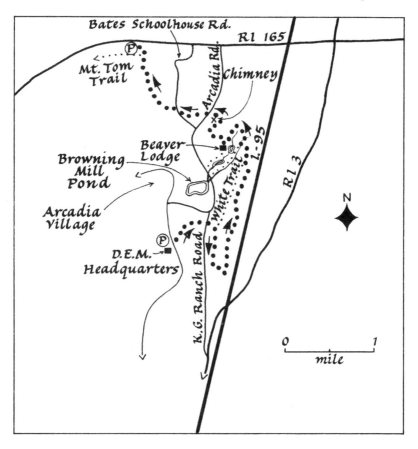

A chimney from some vanished industry baffles walkers of the Arcadia Trail.

passing through an opening in a stone wall, the path forks. Be careful here. The yellow trail makes an abrupt right turn. The more worn fork, going left, is marked in white. It is considered a shortcut path because it links up with the yellow trail again, so you have a choice. However, you will miss quite a lot by taking the shortcut.

The yellow trail, so little used that you have to look closely in places to be sure you're still on it, follows low ridges and wanders a long way through attractive, rocky woods. It crosses numerous seasonal brooks, which run highest in early spring when they are usually decorated with marsh marigolds, skunk cabbages, and other plants at a time when the rest of the forest is still winter-brown.

You'll cross the first of several boulder fields before jumping a stream and climbing over a stone wall. Then the trail makes a sharp left onto an old lane, and a right into a grove of red pines. This grove obviously was planted many years ago; the trees are lined up like soldiers marching in formation.

The detour into the pines is pleasant but brief. You will soon return to the lane and then enter a clearing. This is another tricky spot. The lane runs through the clearing, curving right. The yellow blazes, however, turn left. In this clearing you can find a cellar hole, and just a few yards up the yellow trail is a stone bridge and small, man-made pond—all reminders that this spot once was home to somebody.

For the next 1½ miles the trail roams in and out of pine groves, crosses several areas of boulders that might be difficult for short legs to handle, visits dilapidated bridges and walkways built by a youth conservation group in the 1970s, and cuts through a lovely section of hardwoods where, in spring, you should see many wildflowers, among them bluets, violets, wood anemones, spring beauties, and wild geraniums. This section is lovely in fall too, with a mixture of maples, beeches, and oaks that provide colorful foliage.

For a short distance you will be walking parallel to I-95, and you can hear the traffic on your right, although only in winter can you see it. When the trail curves left, away from the highway, you'll begin seeing cairns—stone mounds built on top of boulders. Who built them and why? With thousands of rocks still scattered about, it doesn't seem that the cairns were built in an effort to clear the land. They give you something to think about as you walk.

In this area you will be reunited with the shortcut white path, which joins you from the left. In another ¼ mile you will emerge onto a gravel road. If your goal is Browning Mill Pond, you can turn left on this road and soon be finished with your walk of about 4 miles.

The yellow trail, however, turns right on the gravel road and runs into what once was a campground. Where the trail turns left into the woods, you may notice faded white blazes going to the right. They lead to the abandoned Dawley State Park on RI 3, where the original Arcadia Trail began years ago.

Following the yellow blazes, you will pass through a pleasant forest punctuated with boulders and brooks. Old wooden walkways carry you over wet areas before the trail curves toward a small pond. The area near this pond is sometimes flooded by beavers; as you walk, keep an eye out for a large beaver lodge built on the near shore. A narrow side path goes to the lodge, allowing for close inspection.

Just beyond the lodge the trail splits. A path goes straight ahead toward the pond's dike and out to Arcadia Road and Browning Mill Pond. The yellow blazes turn right into a grove of tall pines.

After passing the pines the trail goes through a section filled with briars and underbrush. It nearly goes out to the highway, then curves back inland. At one point you can see a large brick chimney in the woods on the left. The chimney does not appear to be from a house or cabin—more likely, it was from some kiln or furnace—and there is just as much speculation among hikers about its origin as there is about the stone cairns passed earlier.

The trail emerges onto Arcadia Road, crosses it, returns to woods briefly, then breaks out onto a dirt road called Bates Schoolhouse Road. You will follow this road only briefly too, for the yellow blazes soon turn onto a barred fire lane identified by a signpost as Bald Hill Trail.

This lane is one of my favorite segments of the walk. It is open and easy to walk, and birds and flowers are usually common here. The forest on both sides is hilly and rocky, and in spring dogwood blossoms add dazzling white decorations. Along this lane you'll also see a miniature stone-walled reservoir, one of the "water holes" built for fire protection in the 1930s.

Just beyond the water hole the trail leaves the lane, going to the right. You will be on the final leg of the walk. This segment features low stone walls, boulders of every size and shape, and a fine mixture of trees. In a low area you'll see a white-blazed trail going left (this is the Mount Tom Trail, although not the part of that trail described in Walk 18). A short distance beyond the intersection you will reach RI 165 and your car.

21. Wickaboxet Trail

A prime wildlife walk and a climactic vista of the state's forgotten area

Hiking distance: 5 miles
Hiking time: 2½ hours

O nly the most knowledgeable of Rhode Island outdoorsmen know Wickaboxet Management Area. It lies in a remote part of the state and has been virtually forgotten; yet it can be a marvelous place to walk.

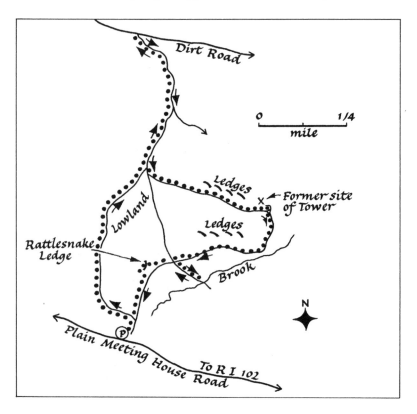

Wickaboxet, the smallest of the state management areas (405 acres), is in West Greenwich, just south of the Coventry line. It was the first state forest and once was extensively used for picnics and other outdoor recreation, but in recent years it has been overshadowed by the much larger Arcadia Management Area a few miles south.

These days only a few hunters use the place in autumn, and occasionally horseback riders use the old roads. Young people sometimes climb the area's featured attraction, Rattlesnake Ledge, but for the most part, Wickaboxet has been left to the grouse, squirrels, deer, and songbirds.

There are no marked hiking trails. Instead you will follow the woods roads. The 5-mile route described here runs the entire length of the state property, then returns to the interior for a stroll past rock ledges, and finally finishes with a climactic climb up Rattlesnake Ledge. No, you aren't likely to find any rattlesnakes; they've been gone for decades.

ACCESS

To reach the entrance to Wickaboxet, drive RI 102 to Plain Meeting House Road, then go west for 3 miles. A sign and a small parking area are on the right side of the road.

TRAIL

The entrance road is gated and forks almost immediately beyond the gate. Inside the fork, hidden in brush, is a small cellar hole.

Unless you are interested only in Rattlesnake Ledge, take the left fork. It is an easy, open lane that runs slightly uphill as it curves to the right. After the turn, you'll see faded double white blazes in the woods on your left; they mark Wickaboxet's boundary.

The forest is fairly open, although recently a great many young pines have begun filling the understory. Birds abound. In the deeper woods you are likely to see flycatchers, woodpeckers, thrushes, warblers, and others. As you progress into areas where the trees are smaller and bushes more abundant, your companions may be waxwings, thrashers, towhees, and grosbeaks. There will be squirrels and chipmunks along the trail too, and occasionally you may come upon a grouse dusting itself on the lane. Deer frequently use this road as well, so you can expect to see their tracks.

Before you have gone 1 mile, your road will merge with another one coming in from the right. Continue walking north. The lane winds back and forth over low, sandy ridges, passing dense groves of thriving young pines, for some distance before you reach a barway. Just beyond this barrier, the lane runs onto a dirt road called Welsh Hollow Road on old maps. Welsh Hollow Road is an inviting road, but land in both directions is private property, so turn around and return on the sandy lane you just walked.

Retrace your steps as far as the Y intersection. Take the left fork, then turn left again almost immediately at another junction. You will be on a lane, flanked by tall trees, that runs along some low rock ledges. At the end of a rocky ridge you'll see a side trail that curls uphill to the left. Take it. It dead-ends atop the ridge at a spot where a fire tower once stood. All that remain are a few concrete anchors.

After this brief detour, resume following the road as it swings downhill, running below another section of ledges. When you reach a crossroads, take a look at the lane to the left. It is grassy and shady—most inviting. I walked it once, intending only to check out a small brook that crosses the road, and was rewarded with the sighting of a large deer that leaped up and bounded through the forest, flashing its white flag of a tail at me.

Just beyond the crossroads, along the main lane, look to the right. Not far off the road looms a massive rock outcropping—Rattlesnake Ledge. While you are not likely to find rattlesnakes, be careful anyway when climbing to the top of this ridge. A fall could be just as painful as a snakebite.

It's best to climb around the right end of the ledge. The view from the top is delightful and surprising after walking more than 4 miles over relatively level terrain. You can see for miles over the treetops; in fact, your view is of what appears to be unbroken forest, possibly the longest such vista still available in Rhode Island.

After descending from the cliff, return to the road. It will be only a short distance, to the right, to your car.

22. Trestle Trail

Two loop walks along an abandoned railroad bed and country roads to observe wildlife

Trestle East: 6 miles, 2½–3 hours
Trestle West: 4½ miles, 2 hours

Trestle Trail in Coventry has undergone several changes since its inception in the 1970s, and more are planned. In recent years this path, which runs about 7 miles along an abandoned railroad bed from Coventry Center to the Connecticut line, has deteriorated considerably. Now there are plans in the works for rebuilding the trail, possibly even paving it so that bicyclists, as well as hikers and horseback riders, can enjoy it.

Until that happens, I recommend breaking the trail into two

Once trains rumbled over the high trestle for which the Trestle Trail was named.

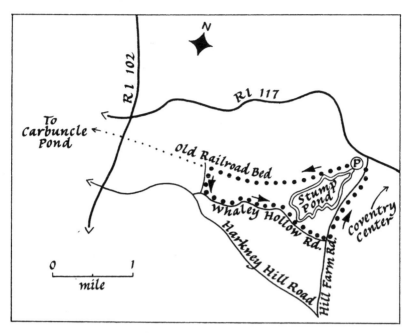

walks, skipping the middle segment near RI 102, where a major quagmire has developed. That section is now underwater much of the year.

These two walks enable you to see most of the original Trestle Trail's highlights, including a pond and surging forests on the eastern end and another lovely pond and the trestle for which the trail was named on the western end. Other reminders of the old railroad are disappearing, but the sharp-eyed can find stone embankments, a few discarded ties, and perhaps some telegraph poles, now all but swallowed up by the forest. By looping back on quiet rural roads, you'll pass fields, meadows, and marshes where you are likely to see wildlife ranging from songbirds and squirrels to deer and otters, while eliminating the need for a second car.

Trestle East

ACCESS

Drive RI 117 into Coventry, then turn south onto Hill Farm Road in the village of Coventry Center. Almost immediately you'll see a

102

gravel parking area beside on a pond on the right. You will start and finish your walk here.

TRAIL

On the left is Coventry Reservoir, a popular fishing spot often called Stump Pond, and on the right is a tiny pond where bullfrogs and swallows are likely to be found in summer. The path, barred to large vehicles by concrete blocks, runs between the ponds.

You will cross a bridge, then begin experiencing one of the problems of this trail: The surface undulates considerably, creating a roller-coaster effect that can make walking tiring. Still, there is much to see. Forest crowding in on both sides creates a virtual tunnel of greenery. Expect to see, or at least hear, thrushes, catbirds, flycatchers, towhees, jays, orioles, and other birds if you visit in spring or summer. On one summer walk here I came across a family of crested flycatchers and a family of orioles, and I was treated to the sight of a brilliant scarlet tanager and its olive, nearly yellow, mate drinking from a water puddle almost at my feet.

In about 1½ miles, you will reach a brook where the old bridge was recently removed. Going down to the water on the left and crossing on the rocks is quite easy and gives you an up-close look at the large blocks of stone used in building railroad bridges.

In another ½ mile, or about 2 miles from your start, you will reach a crossroad, with a dirt lane on the right and a paved street on the left. This is a good place to leave the old railroad bed, because the muddy section near RI 102 is a short distance ahead.

Instead, turn left and walk the paved road uphill past several homes. In less than ½ mile you'll reach a road angling in from the left. This is Whaley Hollow Road. Going straight ahead would soon take you to a highway—Harkney Hill Road—so turn left on Whaley Hollow Road.

The first section is developed with a number of homes, but before long you are likely to see more chipmunks and squirrels than people, and then the pavement gives way to dirt. You'll pass brooks, fields, and an attractive farm on a most pleasant walk before the road returns to pavement just before you reach Hill Farm Road.

Turn left on Hill Farm Road for the final segment, which again takes you past Stump Pond. In slightly more than 1 mile on this road, you will be back at your car.

Trestle West

ACCESS

Drive RI 14 or RI 117 into western Coventry. The two highways merge just east of the Moosup River. From this junction, continue west for 1 mile, and look for a sign for the Carbuncle Pond Fishing Area on the left. Follow the entrance road to its end, and park in one of the small lots near the pond's boat ramp.

TRAIL

Take a footpath that runs around the boat ramp—which actually is a portion of the entrance road flooded by beavers years ago—and follow the shoreline. When you reach a former beach area (a guardrail and metal slide remain), look for a wide path that goes straight ahead into the woods.

This path runs along a shallow marsh, often filled with ducks in fall and swallows in spring. It has a great water lily cover in summer, and I've seen beavers and otters in the marsh. Also, your chances of seeing deer tracks on this sandy path are very good.

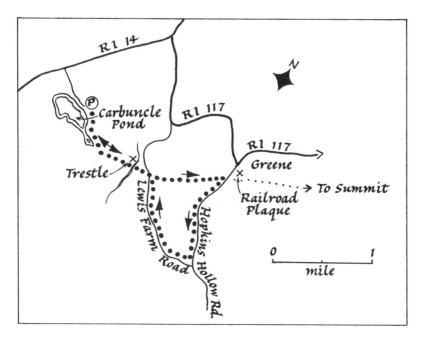

In less than ½ mile you will reach the old railroad bed, which resembles a high ridge. Turn left. A short distance ahead is the trestle, now a footbridge hanging high over the Moosup River. This is a lovely spot, with the picturesque stream below and fields and woods spread out beyond. Just before the bridge, on the left, you may be able to see a couple of the old telegraph poles. These poles once stood guard over railroad tracks; now they are all but obliterated by much taller trees.

Continue walking east. You will quickly cross a gravel road—Lewis Farm Road—which you will later return on, and then go into one of the "green tunnels" now common along the Trestle Trail. There are some stone retaining walls in this segment but little else to remind you that this was once a railroad bed. Now it's simply a straight, easy lane through the forest.

In less than 2 miles from your start you will reach a paved road at the village of Greene. Continue across the road a few yards to see a little monument to the vanished railroad. Below a set of train wheels, painted silver, is a plaque that gives a brief history of the railroad line and Greene.

Return to the paved road—Hopkins Hollow Road—and turn south (now on your left). You'll pass houses, farms, and a youth camp on this road before leaving it in just over 1 mile. Take the first gravel road to the right. This is Lewis Farm Road, which will take you back to the Trestle Trail.

Lewis Farm Road is as delightful to walk as most woods trails. Several homes have been built here in recent years, but the road is still a quiet place where you are as likely to see wildlife as people. I came across a deer fawn on this road, and more than once I've seen quail and grouse dusting themselves in the loose gravel. This road is expected to become part of the long-planned North–South Trail that will run the length of the state, and it's easy to see why it was chosen.

When you again reach the former railroad bed, turn left for the walk back across the trestle to your car at Carbuncle Pond.

23. Parker Woodland– Coventry

A walk to old farms and mills and to mysterious cairns deep in the woods

Hiking distance: 3 miles
Hiking time: 2–2½ hours

A walk through Parker Woodland is a stroll through history. It enables you to take a look at the Rhode Island of 200 years ago in the stone remains of mills, farmhouses, and other buildings as well as mysterious stone cairns.

This trail is the Coventry Tract of Parker Woodland, a large and increasingly popular area owned by the Audubon Society of Rhode Island. The refuge also spills over into Foster (Walk 24).

Parker Woodland lies along Maple Valley Road in an area where farms were abandoned long ago and the land has been reclaimed by forest. Once, the area was a lively—and deadly—place. Two taverns along the old road were known for the ruffians they attracted, and tales of shootings punctuate the region's history and lore. Some local residents still speak of troubled spirits roaming the older houses. Now, however, Parker Woodland is quiet, almost eerie, with many reminders of the past silently reposing beside and beneath vigorous saplings and bushes.

ACCESS

To reach the Coventry Tract, turn east from RI 102 onto Maple Valley Road. The first house on the left is the refuge's headquarters, and there is a parking lot just beyond. For this walk, however, drive about ¼ mile farther down Maple Valley Road until you reach Parking Lot No. 2, also on the left. You will find a large trail sign etched into a wooden sign.

TRAIL

You will immediately come face to face with history. At the trail's start you'll see a sign describing what a team of archaeologists from

Brown University found in 1983, when they explored a home site on the spot. They also studied two charcoal processing sites farther down the trail and a large farm that once prospered far back in the woods. Signs at those sites also provide insight into life in the area in the eighteenth century.

You will pass the charcoal pits quickly and then cross Turkey Meadow Brook before reaching the main, blue-blazed trail. Go left and in just a few minutes you will reach the cairns—dozens of them—scattered through the woods.

The archaeologists did not attempt to solve the mystery of the stone cairns, and perhaps it's better this way. Now each walker can speculate on just who built the pyramid-shaped monuments, and why. Were they built by American Indians for burial or for religious rituals? Or by pre-Columbian explorers who were marking their way by the stars? Or simply by some fussy farmer who wasn't

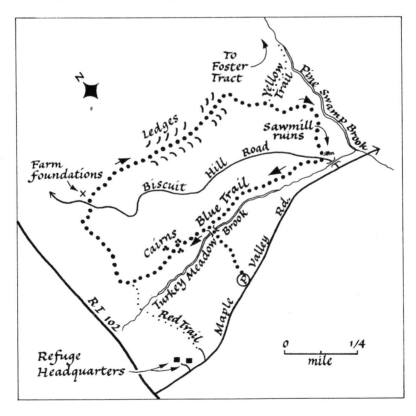

The mysterious stone cairns of Parker Woodland have never been explained.

satisfied with just throwing the rocks onto a pile?

Take time to look over the cairns and note their workmanship, while theorizing on their origins. Many are filled with stones so meticulously fitted together they are still solid after more than two centuries. Restrict your study to looking, however; Audubon allows no disturbing of the cairns.

The trail remains rocky as it loops through magnificent groves of beech trees. At one point you will pass a red-marked side trail (which runs to the Parker headquarters on Maple Valley Road), then the blue trail begins swinging to the right. The walking is easier here for some distance, until you reach the old farm.

You will first find the foundation of a barn. Then, on the opposite side of a dirt road lined on both sides by stone walls, you'll see the cellar hole for the house, the remains of a small outbuilding, and the family's stone-lined well. A sign provides substantial background on the farm, including dates and names.

The dirt road you will cross—Biscuit Hill Road—is a shortcut back to Turkey Meadow Brook, and many walkers use it, possibly as much for its own history as for the steps it saves. Biscuit Hill Road supposedly received its name when a wagon load of biscuits meant for Rochambeau's army was spilled here during the American Revolution. If you take the rocky road to the right, you will reach the brook at an old sawmill site.

The main trail, however, returns to the woods through the "backyard" of the farmhouse and circles through an extremely rocky area. You will pass ledges and boulders of various sizes and shapes, gradually working your way downhill.

A yellow-marked trail breaks off to the left at an immense boulder. This is the connector path to the Foster Tract of Parker Woodland, and it is worth walking because it runs through a beautiful rocky area beside a brook. This is Pine Swamp Brook, and you will be walking upstream, advancing along a series of falls and pools. (See Walk 24 for a description of the forest beyond the brook.)

When you return to the blue trail, go left. You will climb through woods to the end of Biscuit Hill Road, this time emerging near the impressive stone remains of the sawmill, just to your left. Most of the dam still stands, although the center has been removed. Extensive, flat-faced stonework shows the flume and sluiceway that carried the water under the road, where it dropped into a deep cellarlike excavation—again lined with flat stones—that held the huge waterwheel.

This was originally a vertical sawmill, but around 1908, after most of the virgin timber of the area had been harvested, it was altered for a steam-powered saw. A mess hall, bunkhouse, and horse barn were added, and their foundations also remain.

From this point, return to the blue trail, and follow it left along Turkey Meadow Brook. In less than ¼ mile, you will be back at the bridge just downhill from the parking lot.

24. Parker Woodland– Foster

A forest walk through former farmland and beside stone quarries

Hiking distance: 4½ miles
Hiking time: 2½–3 hours

The Foster Tract of Parker Woodland is not nearly as well known—and therefore as well used—as its neighbor the Coventry Tract (Walk 23), but it is a gem in its own right. Officially renamed the Milton A. "Hank" Goudey Memorial Trail in 1992 for the man who served as a volunteer caretaker for 30 years, this trail loops through one-time farmland now returned to forest. You will pass numerous stone walls, several cellar holes and foundations of vanished buildings, and a small stone quarry. On the 3-hour, 4½-mile route described here, you will also visit a picturesque brook that tumbles down a rocky ravine.

ACCESS

The Foster Tract has its own starting point and parking lot, but access can be difficult because of long drives on gravel and dirt roads. I recommend starting and ending at Parking Lot No. 2 for the Coventry Tract. This way you'll hit some of the historical highlights of that walk as well as use the short connector trail between the two tracts. The connector is among the prettiest areas of the entire Parker Woodland.

If you want to walk only the 2.3-mile Foster Trail, you can enter from Old Plainfield Pike about 1 mile east of RI 102. Take gravel Pierce Road south until its end, then go right and continue as the gravel turns to dirt. Old maps show this as Pig Hill Road. The parking area is another mile into the forest.

TRAIL

For those who start at Parking Lot No. 2 off Maple Valley Road, take a few minutes to look over the signs at the archaeological digs at an old homesite and, farther along the trail, a charcoal processing site. Then cross Turkey Meadow Brook and take the blue-blazed trail to the right. (A yellow-blazed trail runs more directly to the Foster Tract, but it is less interesting.) The blue trail follows the brook until it crosses a woods road—Biscuit Hill Road—and passes the remains of a sawmill a few yards to the right. (Both the road and the mill site are described in Walk 23.) The trail goes into a rocky area, swings near a tiny stream called Pine Swamp Brook, and goes back uphill briefly before reaching the connector trail with a sign that reads "To Foster Tract" just beyond an immense boulder.

Go right on the connector (the yellow blazes are not easy to see in autumn, when much of the underbrush is yellow and golden-brown). The path returns to Pine Swamp Brook, which tumbles down a ravine filled with jumbled boulders. It's an appealing area, particularly

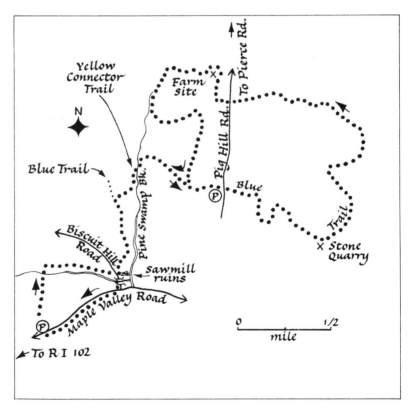

A tumbling brook on the connector trail between the Coventry and Foster tracts of Parker Woodland is one of the loveliest spots in the forest.

where the path drops to the water's edge, enabling you to advance upstream. The brook is a series of falls and pools. When you see a low rock dam that creates a larger pool, it's time to cross the brook. There is a bridge, but in most seasons the brook above the pool is so narrow you can step over it on the boulders.

Still on the yellow trail, you will soon leave the brook, climb uphill, and in a matter of minutes reach the intersection with the Foster Tract Trail, marked in blue. Turn right here, and you will quickly arrive at the parking lot along Pig Hill Road.

Cross the road, passing through a brushy area, and you will soon be heading downhill. After some distance, you'll see a rugged ledge on the left with several small caves at its foot, and you'll enter a pleasant, open section of woods as you skirt a small swamp.

Off the trail, to the right, is an area of broken and piled stones, left over from quarry operations, and when the leaves are down you'll be able to see the foundation of a building. It is worth inspecting.

From this point the trail curves left and the walking alternates from descents through rocky lowlands to hilly but easy woodlands for considerable distance. You'll see signs that mark the refuge's boundary, and later you'll pass a three-sided stone foundation and cross Pig Hill Road for the second time.

After passing through a grove of tall pines—one of the few areas in this second-growth forest where you find mature trees—you will reach the "fields" of a vanished farm. Boundaries are still marked by stone walls, some high and straight, others little more than tumbledown piles. You'll pass one small cellar hole, probably a barn or outbuilding, then swing through a break in a wall, curl around to the left, and reach a virtual network of walls.

Across the wall on your left is the cellar hole of the farmhouse. Taking up half of its cellar space is the huge foundation for the chimney. On the far side are the steps, and there is a tree growing exactly where the long-ago farmers climbed in and out of the cellar. Out a few yards from the stairway, hidden beneath a huge flat stone, is the family's well. Its circular, stone-lined walls are a work of art and invite inspection, but be very careful—old wells can be dangerous.

From the farm site, the trail drops down a steep hill, curves left, and runs near Pine Swamp Brook again. Just before you reach the brook, you'll pass, on your left, a stone fireplace built against a boulder. The rocks, green with lichens, hint of being there for ages. Was it part of a cabin or merely the project of somebody camping for the night? Nobody knows.

When you climb out of the brook's valley, you'll be back in second-growth woods—mostly oaks—and will pass numerous stone walls that seem bewildering. They wander at all angles and few are connected—just lines of rocks for some distance, then they end. They are probably simply a means of clearing some of the fields of rocks.

At the fork with the yellow connector trail, turn right and return to your car in the Coventry lot. When you reach the bridge at the mill site at the bottom of Biscuit Hill Road, you can go out onto Maple Valley Road and finish your walk on the paved roadway.

25. Gainer Dam

An excellent walk for birders and a view of the Gainer
Dam and Scituate Reservoir

Hiking distance: 2.8 miles
Hiking time: 1½ hours

T his walk is different. Unlike most of the hikes in this book, this
one is on pavement all the way, and you are strictly forbidden
from wandering off into the surrounding woodlands. Still, it is a

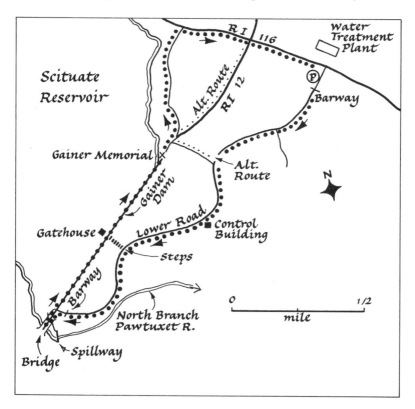

charming stroll that can be as short as slightly more than 1 mile or stretched out to almost 3 miles.

One of the few walks in the central part of Rhode Island, this route takes you across the massive Gainer Memorial Dam that created the vast Scituate Reservoir and loops through a quiet area of forest and grass on a road closed to vehicular traffic. In most seasons, it is an excellent walk for birders, offering glimpses of field birds (robins, meadowlarks, killdeer), woods birds (chickadees, nuthatches, thrushes), and lake birds (mergansers, ducks, geese). It is particularly inviting in early spring, when many migrating waterfowl stop over on the reservoir, a time when many other trails are too muddy for pleasant walking.

Because reservoir land is off-limits to everyone, wildlife is thriving. Without leaving the roads, I've seen otters, raccoons, and numerous chipmunks and squirrels, plus wild turkeys and grouse, in addition to waterfowl and songbirds.

ACCESS

The walk's start is located on RI 116 just south of RI 12 in Scituate. Look for a barred road directly across from a large water treatment plant. There is ample parking space on the road before the barway. If you arrive on a weekend morning, you will be likely to find several cars here as this has become an increasingly popular place for joggers and walkers.

TRAIL

To the right, as you pass the barway, is one of the open, lawnlike fields of grass you will see on this walk. On one recent spring morning I counted 24 robins strutting about within 50 feet of my path. On the left is a stand of pine trees in precise rows, obviously planted as part of the reservoir project.

On both sides of the roadway you will see yellow signs that warn "No Trespassing: Fishing, Boating, Picnicking, Skating, Bathing, Trapping, Hunting, Smoking, Building Fires, and Any Act Tending to Pollute the Waters or to Injure the Property are Prohibited. Violators will be Prosecuted."

But walking is permitted here, as long as you don't wander off the road. It is one of the few places anywhere on the 13,000-acre reservoir property, other than public highways, where even walking is allowed.

The road runs below the dam and provides access to a control

115

building. In 1 mile, this road will take you to the far (western) end of the dam and beside the reservoir spillway. Because there is virtually no reservoir business conducted on weekends, the road is ideal for walkers and joggers.

Almost as soon as you begin your walk you can see that the area was farmed before being taken for the reservoir in 1915. Stone walls still march across the hills, and there are several abandoned roadways visible in the forest, including one that crosses a small brook on a stone bridge just to the left of your road. Six entire villages as well as numerous farms vanished when the land was turned into a reservoir.

In less than ½ mile you will reach a road junction. A turn to the right would take you to RI 12 at the eastern end of the dam. This is the route that many walkers take after crossing the dam. A turn left downhill, however, will enable you to walk the full length of the lower road.

Fences line most of the middle segment of the lower road. To the

The lower road below Gainer Dam is an excellent place for an easy stroll.

116

right, high above you, is the dam with RI 12 running along its crest. The entire bank from the highway down to the lower road is grass, a great place for robins and similar birds. At one point, you'll reach a long set of stairs that run from your road all the way up to the old gatehouse at the center of the dam. Now, though, the stairs are barred and a sign reads "No Trespassing."

When trees again close in on both sides, you will be starting the uphill curve toward the highway. Through the trees on the left you can see the deep channel for the spillway water before seeing the spillway itself. When you reach the highway, at another barway, take a few moments and walk left to a bridge over the spillway. When the reservoir is full, the roar and spray of the falls are worth a bit of lingering.

As you turn back and start walking along the highway across the dam, the view to your left is that of a forested lake. Rocky shorelines and pine and spruce forests give the reservoir a picturesque aura. To your right, far below, is the roadway you walked earlier.

You can walk on either side of the highway. Old-fashioned stone walls run the length of the dam on each side, and sandy paths follow the highway on both sides between the walls and the pavement. It is slightly more than ½ mile across the dam, and along the way you will pass the old gatehouse built in 1926.

At the eastern end of the dam, on the left side, is a large concrete and bronze tribute to Joseph Gainer, who was mayor of Providence when the reservoir was built. A plaque states that water storage was begun in 1925 and distribution of the water started a year later. Some walkers park here and make the shortest dam-and-lower-road circuit by way of the shortcut road you passed earlier. The shortcut, now fenced against vehicular travel, runs off the right side of the highway nearly across from the Gainer monument. Walking only this short loop would make a hike of just over 1 mile.

If you take this short connector to the lower road and return to your car, your walk will be about 2 miles. If you continue eastward on RI 12 to RI 116, then turn right and walk to your car, you will travel about 2½ miles. However, I like to make the trip a bit longer, so I turn left just beyond the monument on a road that follows the reservoir to RI 116. There is no signpost on this road, but this was part of the original Scituate Avenue, a name now used on the straightened RI 12.

An earthen dike runs along the left side of this road and a dense woods is on the right. There is little traffic, and sometimes the road

117

seems to be paved with acorns and pine cones, but you can see evidence that this road is open to cars—unlike the lower road, which is closed to cars, you're likely to see litter.

Shortly after passing a small cemetery on your right, you will reach RI 116. Turn right. A boggy area, complete with skunk cabbage and other swamp plants, will be on your right, and a woods filled with ledges and stones will be on your left.

In a matter of minutes you will reach RI 12. Cross it and head downhill toward your car. Chances are the robins will still be in the grassy field where you began.

26. Durfee Hill

A stroll to Killingly Pond on the border of Rhode Island and Connecticut

Hiking distance: 9 miles
Hiking time: 4–4½ hours

W alking from Durfee Hill to Killingly Pond and back is a 9-mile stroll, one of the longest in this book, but it seems far shorter. Not only is it easy and relatively level, but there is enough to see along the way to keep you interested.

The walk begins in a state management area, circles around a small pond, crosses a highway, then wanders for miles through a superb forest before reaching Killingly Pond, most of which is in Connecticut. The return trip, also through forest, follows a different trail that visits a unique network of stone walls, then curls along a gravel road for a look at a gristmill before returning to woods along a high, rugged ledge.

A note of caution, however: This is not a blazed trail, and numerous side paths can make it confusing. It may be best to make this walk with a hiking club or somebody who knows the area before attempting it on your own.

While the vast forest would make this a pleasing walk in autumn, the area teems with hunters then. Instead, go in spring or early summer. The abundance of evergreen trees also makes it a charming walk in winter, but this section receives more snow than most areas, sometimes too much for enjoyable walking.

ACCESS

To reach the start, drive US 44 in Glocester almost to the Connecticut line, turning south on RI 94 across from Bowdish Reservoir. Follow RI 94 1.3 miles to a hunter checking station, on the left, in the Durfee Hill Management Area. You can park beside the building.

TRAIL

From the parking area, look over the surrounding countryside.

119

Below and to the right, as you face the station building, lies a small pond. Begin by circling this pond, going left on a faint lane in front of the building. It runs downhill, past the small fields planted for the benefit of wildlife.

The lane curves away from the pond briefly, then starts back. As it begins curving back toward the right along a narrow field, look for a path going into the woods on the opposite (left) side of this field strip. You may have to watch closely—this path is easy to miss.

Take the path into the woods. It will immediately cross a tiny brook on a pile of rocks, then go slightly uphill as it continues curling around the pond. For much of this section, you will be walking through dense hemlocks, which all but hide the pond from view.

As you emerge from a hemlock grove and the main trail starts descending to the right, look for a cutoff on the left that drops into a small ravine. Take the cutoff; it quickly leads to RI 94. If you miss the

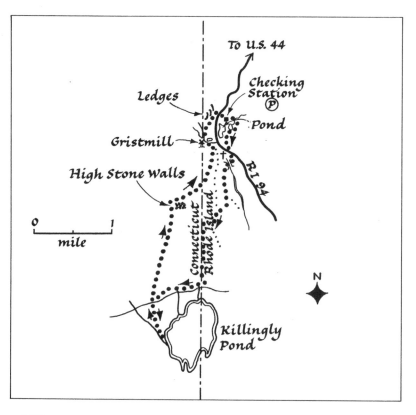

cutoff, and you find yourself on the pond's earthen dike, simply follow a lane left to the highway.

Once on RI 94, go left a short distance, passing a small cemetery on your right, until you reach utility pole No. 92. Reenter the woods, on the right, on a trail that begins by a guardrail.

The trail drops quickly downhill. You'll step over one tiny brook, then have to cross a larger stream. At present, one log is all that remains of a bridge, although a section of the old bridge is downstream to the right and can still be used.

The trail is somewhat rocky through this area but easy to walk. Azaleas and laurel brighten the route when in bloom, but the dominant tree is the hemlock. Hemlocks of all sizes can be found so often that some hiking clubs refer to this route as the Hemlock Trail.

At the first path junction after you cross the stream, about 1.6 miles from your start, go right. (The way left soon leaves state property.) At the next junction, after passing stone walls and an obscure cellar hole, turn left. (Turning right on this one will take you away from Killingly Pond.)

The next section of trail is deeply rutted in places, and you'll have to cross some wet areas before emerging—about 3 miles from your start—on a gravel lane. Turn right.

Stay on the lane for more than ½ mile. You'll cross into Connecticut in this segment, while walking parallel to Killingly Pond. Ignore cutoffs to the left—they are on private property—and enjoy this quiet, shady section where red squirrels far outnumber people.

After you begin seeing Connecticut state property signs on both sides, begin looking for a lane to the left, barred with green metal posts and a metal pole. There are similar posts on a lane going right; that lane will be your return route.

Go left on the barred lane. It runs downhill to a gravel road, which you can take a short distance left to the pond. The pond is about 4½ miles from your start, the halfway mark, and is an excellent place for a lunch break. Although undeveloped, it is a popular place for fishing, swimming, picnicking, and small-boat activity.

When you are ready to resume walking, go back up the gravel road and the dirt lane. Pass the green-posted barway, cross the roadway you walked earlier, and follow the other barred path, now straight ahead. This is an open and easy-to-walk lane.

Again, you have to disregard side trails and stay on the main path. For much of this segment there are low stone walls on one side or the other,

121

or on both sides. There are fewer hemlocks here; you'll find instead a good mixture of hardwoods, including a great many young chestnuts.

At the Y fork in the trail bear right. The path then winds around for a distance before reaching a network of unusually high stone walls, running at what seems like erratic angles through the woods. Take a few moments to check out the stonework; it apparently is from a long-vanished barn and livestock compound.

Beyond the walls the trail makes a sharp right turn and then weaves downhill to a gravel road. To the right, just a few yards away, is RI 94; if you're tired, you can take 94 to the left back to your car, making a walk of about 8 miles.

A single log is all that remains of one bridge on the Durfee Hill Trail.

You would, however, be missing two of the trip's highlights. Instead, turn left on the gravel road, then quickly right on another gravel road that goes to a bridge. The building on the far end of the bridge is the old gristmill. You can take a path down from the near end of the bridge to look over the stonework virtually under the bridge. The waterwheel is gone but much of the dam and sluice remain. And when you pass the building, you can see a large round millstone lying in the yard.

Continue walking up the road, past a house on the right, until you reach the first lane going off into the woods on the right. Follow this lane, carpeted with pine needles, as it goes uphill, then around the right side of a swampy area.

As you approach RI 94, look closely on the left for a narrow path. This side trail will take you along an impressive, rugged rock ledge that looms above you nearly all the way out to RI 94. When you reach the highway, turn left and you'll be back at your car in minutes.

27. Walkabout Trail

Three choices of loops in one walk to ponds, hemlock groves, and a wildlife marsh

Hiking distance: 7½ miles
Hiking time: 3½–4 hours

The Walkabout Trail has undergone several changes in recent years—some good and some bad from a hiker's point of view—but it is still among the more popular trails. It can be a delight under the right conditions.

Although a sign at its start, near Bowdish Reservoir in the Glocester portion of the George Washington Management Area, continues to list the three walking loops as 2, 6, and 8 miles, all are a bit shorter now and there is no longer a plant-identifying nature trail at one end. The three trails begin and end together, and they still take you beside a campground, around a couple of ponds, through dense woodland, and across boggy areas. When you take the widest loop, the 8-mile circuit described here, you will also wander through one of the most impressive hemlock groves in Rhode Island and visit a wildlife marsh.

The Walkabout was cut and named by Australian sailors back in 1965, while their ship, the Perth, was in dry dock in Newport. The name refers to the wanderings of the Australian aborigines.

ACCESS

To reach the trailhead, take US 44 to the George Washington Camping Area, about 4½ miles west of Chepachet. Turn right onto the campground road, and continue 0.3 mile until you reach a lane that runs by the park office on the left. Turn and park along this wide lane.

TRAIL

I've walked these trails in all seasons and feel, without a doubt, that autumn is best. Because the trail runs so near a pond and crosses lowlands, it is likely to be quite muddy or even flooded in spring.

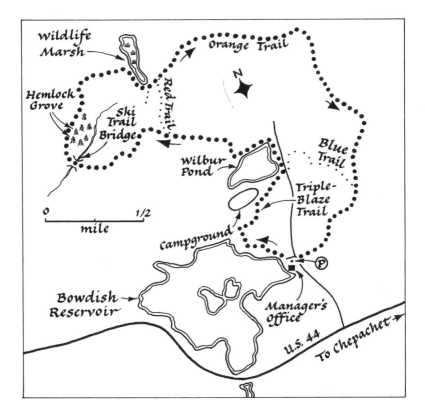

Summer's problems include the crowds from the campground and beach, as well as mosquitoes in the boggy areas, and the rocky terrain can make winter walking very treacherous, although the hemlocks and pines are stunning in snow.

It is difficult to find any drawbacks in fall. I walked the trail once on a sparkling Saturday morning in October and went more than 7 miles without seeing another person. Chickadees and other birds accompanied me all the way. There were chipmunks and red squirrels busy in the trees, and the colors of the mixed forest ranged from gold and orange to deep green. There are also far fewer campers in autumn (the official camping season runs from May 1 to September 30), and no fees are charged for entering the area in fall.

The trails begin behind a large sign near the beach of Bowdish Reservoir. The 8-mile loop is blazed in orange, the 6-mile loop in red, and the 2-mile loop in blue. Following the brightly painted triple

125

blazes, start by walking the reservoir shoreline, a pleasant stroll through laurel, pine, and hemlock with frequent cutoffs to rocky points jutting into the water. There are footbridges over some low spots, the first of many plank bridges you'll find on this trail. The path soon swings right, skirting the campground. This is where the walks

The Walkabout Trail provides many good views of Bowdish Reservoir.

were shortened when the trail was rerouted during an expansion of the camping area.

You'll see some white marks on trees near the campground, but they have nothing to do with the Walkabout. Stay with the triple blazes as the trail briefly runs along a woods lane. When you reach a gravel road, note that only the blue trail continues straight ahead; the orange and red routes swing left into the forest, starting the circuit around Wilbur Pond.

It's a busy pond in summer but tranquil and picturesque in fall. The trail, after some up-and-down scrambling, runs at the pond's very edge, and this is where you may have to detour in high water. You will circle about half of the pond before the trail breaks away and goes uphill to the right into an open, pleasant woodland.

In slightly less than ½ mile, you will reach the sign indicating the red loop turns off to the right. This shortcut passes numerous stone walls and rock piles that show that the area was once farmland and then crosses a brook before rejoining the orange loop. The red trail, which misses the best hemlock groves and the wildlife marsh, is considerably shorter than the advertised 6 miles—it is probably under 5 miles.

Remain on the orange trail, which my pedometer now clocks at 7½ miles, and you will soon reach a number of gravel lanes (popular in winter as snowmobile trails). At most crossings you'll find a bench and trash barrel, more recent improvements. When you cross the third roadway in about ¼ mile, you will find a sign barring unauthorized vehicles on what starts out as a wide, grassy lane.

This lane winds downhill into a dense hemlock area, and the trail quickly narrows. Trees tower above you on both sides and the thick evergreen foliage casts a deep, permanent shadow over the trail. For a brief period you'll walk on a wide, smooth path that crosses a rocky brook on a wooden bridge; this is part of the cross-country ski trail that begins at Peck Pond in nearby Pulaski State Park.

Just beyond the bridge an orange arrow painted on a tree indicates that your trail swings right into the brush. The path is narrow here, and there are several fallen trees to climb past. The trail runs parallel to a gravel road for a considerable distance and then crosses it, leading to a section much easier to walk, even though you are at times returning to rocky footing.

In about ½ mile you will cross another road and almost immediately reach the wildlife marsh. Trees at the water's edge offer veils from which you can observe the marsh inhabitants, mainly muskrats, swallows (in summer), kingfishers, and the colorful wood ducks that are lured by the wooden nesting boxes installed on poles above the water. The trail crosses the earthen dam built to create the marsh and offers a good opportunity to pause and take a good look.

As soon as you cross the dike the trail splits. Go left (the path to the right is unmarked), and you'll soon meet the red-blazed trail coming in from the right. In another ½ mile you will cross your final gravel road and, before long, drop into a lovely but wet area of laurel, hemlocks, and moss, where you may have to pick your way, even in autumn, by stepping on exposed roots.

When you climb out of the damp section, you will be very close to rejoining the blue trail you left miles earlier. It will be only ½ mile, to the left, from the intersection back to your car.

28. Buck Hill

A three-state walk through an area with abundant wildlife

Hiking distance: 4.7 miles   *VISITED 4/29/06*

Hiking time: 2½–3 hours

B uck Hill is one of the places to go to if you want to combine walking with wildlife watching. It offers plenty of both.

The Buck Hill State Management Area is in Burrillville, the extreme northwest corner of the state. Management of this forest has resulted in an abundance of wildlife, both waterfowl and upland game, along with all the songbirds and small animals that such areas attract.

The walk described here runs beside a man-made marsh, through rocky woodlots, and along a grassy road that passes numerous management fields, meadows, and small ponds. In the 4.7-mile loop, you'll also step briefly into Massachusetts and Connecticut, so you can boast of walking in three states in your 2½-hour ramble.

What wildlife you see depends on when you visit and how observant—and lucky—you are. Ducks, owls, hawks, grouse, quail, pheasants, wild turkeys, deer, foxes, rabbits, squirrels, woodchucks, raccoons, dozens of varieties of songbirds, and numerous other creatures inhabit Buck Hill.

ACCESS

To reach the unmarked entrance, take RI 100 north from Pascoag to Buck Hill Road and turn left. Watch your odometer; the entrance is 2.3 miles from the turnoff. You will pass a fire tower and a road for a Boy Scout camp on your left, then a rifle range on the right, before you reach the gravel access road, also on the right.

During most of the year, you can drive only ⅓ mile before being stopped at a barway. On the right you will see signs warning of a rifle range; stay out of that area. During hunting season—fall and early winter—you can continue driving the management roads, but that is Buck Hill's busiest time and the wrong time for walking.

Moving the parking area away from the marsh has made this a

129

slightly longer walk than previously, but it is more pleasant now. Not only is there more wildlife, but the trails and lanes are more open and easier to walk.

TRAIL

Walk straight ahead from the barway on the gravel road. You will see other roads and the first of many tiny ponds with nesting boxes for wood ducks. At an intersection you'll see white blazes along a road coming from the left; that is your return route. Yellow blazes appear on the road going straight ahead. Follow them, and in a few minutes you will reach the large marsh, where there are many more duck houses and hundreds of skeletons of trees killed when a dike was put up to create the marsh. It's an intriguing place, and sometimes a bit

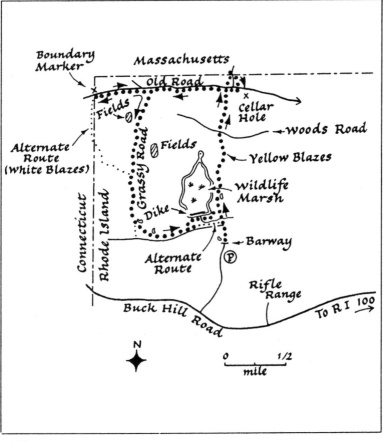

eerie, particularly in early morning when mist rises from the water and in evening when shadows loom.

After taking time to look over the marsh—which usually is alive with swallows, blackbirds, flycatchers, and waxwings, in addition to ducks—follow the yellow blazes around to the right and into the woods. The path narrows considerably and the surface is very rocky. You can still see a bit of orange paint on some of the trees; years ago the blazes were the brightest orange available.

In less than 1 mile from your start you'll reach a woods road. Follow the blazes directly across it. The next section has larger trees, some laurel undergrowth, and a number of stone walls, reminders that this was once farmland. At 1.4 miles you will emerge onto another road, this one an ancient thoroughfare lined by stone walls. Again, the yellow-blazed path goes directly over it. If you continue following the blazes, you will reach the state line border in about 0.1 mile, and you can say you walked to Massachusetts.

Retrace your steps back to the old wagon road, turn left (east), and walk just a few yards. You can find the cellar hole at what is supposed to be the site of the area's first homesteader. In recent years, much of the brush around the cellar has been cleared away and it is now much easier to find. It's on a small knoll, just off the right side of the road.

From the cellar hole, turn around and walk back down the road, past the yellow-marked path you took earlier. There are no blazes

Skeletons of trees can give the marsh at Buck Hill an eerie appearance.

131

along the road but none are needed. It is still an open, easy-to-walk roadway. You will soon reach a wide, grassy lane on the left. The lane leads to the management fields, but if you want to say you've walked to Connecticut, stay on the old road—you can walk the grassy lane later. The stroll to the state boundary and back will add only about ¾ mile to your hike.

Where the road curves right, toward a small open field, look straight ahead. You can see a faint, overgrown lane in the woods, now merely a narrow footpath. Take it. The path is soon joined by a motorcycle trail coming in from the right and then is wider as it goes downhill. Follow it for some distance. After crossing a low stone bridge over a brook, you should see a white-blazed trail crossing your lane. Look on the right for the state boundary marker. It is an upright fieldstone with "RI" chiseled on one side and "C" on the other.

You could take the white-marked trail, to the left, but you would miss nearly 1 mile of the grassy lane, and consequently, much of the wildlife that makes Buck Hill special. Therefore, I recommend backtracking to the lane you passed earlier, now on your right.

You'll immediately see a small pond, on your right, with the inevitable wood-duck house. There are similar ponds ahead and numerous small clearings—fields cut from the forest. Some are planted in grains, some are left in meadows. In spring it's not unusual to hear a quail whistling or a pheasant crowing from these fields, and if you happen by at the right time of day—morning or evening—you might see a deer or fox here. I've also seen woodchucks and rabbits on the trail itself, and at each pool you are likely to find deer tracks and raccoon footprints.

Each field is screened from the lane by trees, and each has an entrance road that enables you to take a look. However, return to the main lane each time. After you have walked nearly 1 mile on the lane, and about 3.7 miles in all, you'll see the white-blazed trail coming in from the right. You'll have the blazes with you the rest of the way back to the gravel road where you began.

Before reaching the gravel road, the grassy lane becomes a sandy woods road that curves considerably. Be sure to look for a narrow path on the left; it leads to the earthen dike at the marsh you saw earlier. If you miss the path, go out to the gravel road and turn left. The dike is a grassy ridge that offers an excellent view of the swamp, and it's the perfect place for a rest stop before heading back to your car.

29. Black Hut

A quiet walk in the woods of northern Rhode Island

Hiking distance: 6 miles
Hiking time: 2½–3 hours

I f you are looking for a quiet woods walk, give Black Hut a try. There you can roam for miles with little chance of running into other hikers and maybe not see any other people at all.

The Black Hut Management Area in Burrillville is one of the more overlooked public forests in Rhode Island. It draws some hunters in

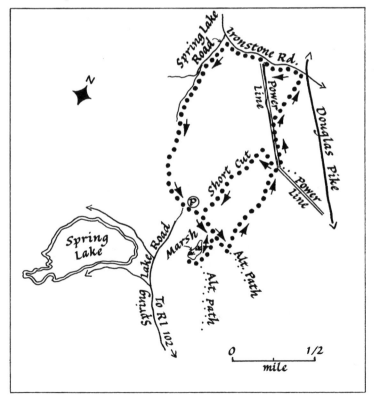

autumn and early winter, and occasionally trail bikers use the access roads, but for most of the year the 1,300-acre forest is virtually forgotten. Just the kind of place many hikers like.

These walks—one is 6 miles, the other is 3 miles—are pleasant but unspectacular. You won't find high rock ledges, deep gorges, or historical attractions. For the most part, you simply stroll through attractive, mixed woods. You'll also pass numerous little fields planted for wildlife and will visit a lovely marsh hidden in the forest, so your chances of seeing animals and birds are good.

A note of caution: These routes are not blazed or marked in any way, so some care must be taken to keep from wandering off on side paths. The 3-mile walk is flat and easy, but the 6-mile hike involves some hill climbing and a stretch of paved and gravel roads.

ACCESS

Black Hut lies almost on the Massachusetts line in Burrillville. Take RI 102 north from Chepachet or south from Slatersville and take the Glendale exit. In the tiny village of Glendale, look for Joslin Road, which passes under RI 102, and take Joslin 0.1 mile north to the first road on the left—Spring Lake Road. Follow Spring Lake, which begins as pavement and eventually turns to dirt, to its end at a parking area in the forest.

TRAIL

Barred lanes run both left and right from the parking area. The lane to the left once was a continuation of Spring Lake Road, and if you are doing the 6-mile route, you will return on this old road. To start your walk, however, take the lane to the right.

The lane is flanked with tall oaks and maples, with a healthy sprinkling of smaller plants such as sassafras and laurel and some young pines and chestnuts. You'll quickly pass a narrow path on the left—this will be your return route if you're doing the 3-mile loop.

In 0.3 mile you will reach a trail junction. To see the marsh take the right fork. This is a delightful segment with tall trees and small fields on the left and the marsh on the right. Look over some of the fields; you might be lucky enough to see a deer, fox, or pheasant.

Most of this part of the marsh is obscured by thick growth, so continue on the lane until you reach the earthen dike that created the marsh. This grassy dam offers good views of the marsh and perhaps of the ducks and other birds that are drawn to it.

A winding lane takes walkers deep into the heart of Black Hut Management Area.

A trail continues beyond the dam but eventually runs off state property and out to Spring Lake Road. To continue this walk, retrace your steps past the fields back to the lane junction you found earlier.

Turn right (left would take you back to your car) on the main lane, which is lined with stone walls. This lane is attractive and easy to walk, but it runs straight through the management area, and if you stay on it, you'll have to turn around and come back. Instead, from the junction, look for the second trail breaking off to the left (the first runs only to a field). This second path, only 0.1 mile from the marsh trail junction, enables you to make both the 3-mile and 6-mile circuits.

The trail is curvy, arched over with trees in some places, and passes still more small fields. When you reach a cleared strip cut through the forest for a power line, you will have gone about 2 miles and you will have a decision to make.

If you are planning to do the 3-mile loop, take a path that runs to the left just before the clearing. This path swings through mixed woods with plenty of laurel bushes all the way back to the entrance lane. When you reach this lane, turn right. You will be just a few yards from your car.

If you want to walk 6 miles, remain on the trail that runs into the power-line clearing. Near the far side of the strip, just before the trail reaches a brook, look for a narrow path going uphill to the left. Before taking the side path, however, you might want to cross the brook and look over an old earthen dike in the woods on the left. The brook was once dammed here, probably for a long-vanished mill.

When you are ready to resume your walk, take the narrow path that runs along the edge of the clearing. You could continue following the clearing until you reach a paved road, but there are several wet areas on the way. A more pleasant alternative is to stay on the power-line path for just a few hundred yards, until you come to a trail going into the woods on the right. Taking this trail makes your walk a little longer, but this woods segment is very pretty with boulders, pines, and ferns.

The trail emerges onto West Ironstone Road, the northern boundary of the state property. Go left on the winding, hilly road. You'll soon pass under the power line, then reach a paved road going left. This is another section of Spring Lake Road. Take it. You'll pass several homes before the road turns to gravel and splits. Take the left fork.

The old road now narrows to a footpath, but the flanking trees have been cut back, allowing a good look at birds that frequent the bushy margin and wildflowers that often grow here. The path runs up and down several rocky slopes before returning you to your car.

30. Diamond Hill

A steep climb to the top and an easy downhill stroll

Hiking distance: 2 miles
Hiking time: 1½ hours

W alking the Diamond Hill Trail has changed several times in recent years, and each change has reduced the mileage considerably. Still, this park in Rhode Island's northeastern corner remains attractive; it's still well worth a visit.

Previously, both sides of steep, rocky Diamond Hill sported skiing operations, and a hiking trail crossed the hill's summit, curled around

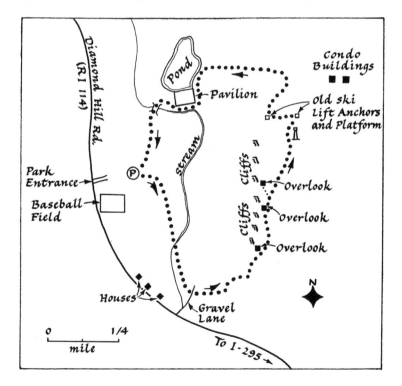

a reservoir, and wandered into Massachusetts. It was a challenging walk that tested the hiker's woodsmanship and physical stamina.

When the ski business fell apart, the state-owned side of the hill was developed into a multifaceted park. The opposite slope—formerly Ski Valley—was developed in another way. It now is crowded with condominiums.

Now, this walk through Diamond Hill State Park is barely 2 miles, but it continues to provide considerable charm. It begins with the challenge of a climb to the top of a rocky cliff that offers panoramic views of the region, then ends with a stroll through a park that adds its own attractions at all times of the year.

Be prepared to spend some time enjoying the park after your walk. There are free concerts in summer, spectacular foliage in autumn, sledding and skating in winter, and trout fishing and kite-flying in spring. The walk described here will take less than 2 hours, but bring along a picnic or sled or kite or fishing rod, and a visit to Diamond Hill can easily wile away most of a day.

ACCESS

Take I-295 into Cumberland, exit on RI 114 (Diamond Hill Road), and follow the road 4 miles to Diamond Hill State Park, which is on the right. It doesn't matter which part of the large parking lot you choose; you will begin by walking to the right and return from the left.

TRAIL

At the right front section of the parking lot you'll find a line of trees bordering a small stream. Walk along this edge of the lot to the right, going through an auxiliary parking lot (usually barred). The stream will be on your left, and you'll see a baseball field on your right.

The stream cuts across your path where the gravel ends, but you can cross the water on large pipes. You will be following an old railroad bed (the tracks were removed long ago), so the trail is straight and level. Continue, while passing behind a few homes, until you reach a gravel lane coming in from RI 114 on the right.

Towering above you on the left will be a 150-foot cliff. Several trails go up the rocks, which are marred by decades of graffiti, but look for the small metal discs nailed to trees. This spot is the southern terminus of the Appalachian Mountain Club's (AMC's) long Warner Trail that runs all the way to Canton, Massachusetts.

Take the trail up to the rim. It's a relatively steep and strenuous

The rugged cliffs of Diamond Hill tower above the surrounding countryside.

climb but not really very dangerous, and you will reach the top in minutes. Now the going gets more tricky. You may have to look hard for metal discs. Ignore all paint markings on rocks and trees and the other paths that weave among the trees.

Take some time to enjoy the view from the rim. Spread out below is Diamond Hill Village, and beyond are hills and forests. You can often watch mountain climbers using this headwall to practice their rappeling techniques.

The disc trail runs along the rim to several rocky outlooks before swerving back into the woods a short distance. Stay on it. When you reach a large water tower, installed for the condominium project below you on the right, go around the left side of the tower. You will soon reach two huge concrete blocks that once served as anchors for the ski lift lines. From these foundations, take a path to the left for several yards to another concrete platform. This was the spot where skiers dismounted for their runs down the hill. Now saplings and young trees are thriving here; they nearly obscure the view.

Follow a path to the right from the platform. It goes a short distance through a grove of young trees and emerges onto a gravel lane. You can go a short distance to the right for a look at the Ski Valley condominium complex and the reservoir beyond, but when you are ready to resume your walk to the park, return to the rim on the left side of the ridge.

The gravel lane will curl down from the summit toward a grassy slope. You'll have to swing around the end of a chain-link fence, but in moments you will be in an area ideal for sledding or kite-flying, and a few more strides will take you to the pond and pavilion where concerts are held in summer. The trout stream is behind and beyond the pavilion, and picnic facilities are all around—you will be ready for the second half of your day in the park. Your car will be in the parking area to your left.

31. Lincoln Woods

A leisurely park stroll around a picturesque pond

Hiking distance: 3 miles
Hiking time: 1½–2 hours

Lincoln Woods is a large, old park close to Rhode Island's population centers, but it is often overlooked by walkers, particularly those who prefer the solitude of so-called wilderness areas. Such people are missing a good thing.

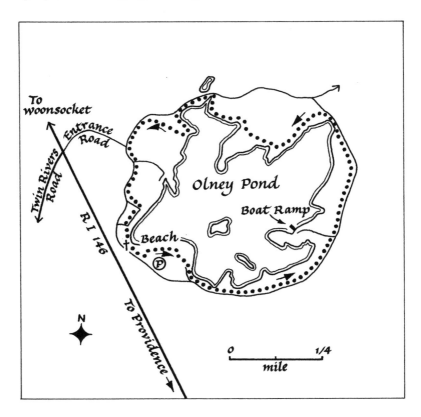

On this easy loop around the park's central feature, picturesque Olney Pond, you will stroll just under 3 miles. You can walk a road all the way if you wish, or you can swing through forest on several occasions. You can try your hand at fishing, take time for a picnic, or even end your walk with a refreshing swim. There are a great many other paths and trails through the woods, but none are blazed and sorting them out can be confusing, so walking around the pond is the recommended route.

The park is a busy place, especially in summer, but in spring and autumn there is plenty of room for walking. You are not likely to see much wildlife, although ducks and songbirds are common, as are squirrels, chipmunks, and muskrats. And there is the sport of people-watching. Along your route you will meet joggers, picnickers, bicy-clists, and families strolling with small children. In some areas there will be fishermen, horseback riders, orienteering competitors, and sunbathers.

ACCESS

The park is in Lincoln, almost within sight of Providence, Pawtucket, North Providence, and Central Falls. Access from both the north and south is provided by RI 146 via Twin Rivers Road. In summer a per-vehicle fee is charged for entering, but there is no charge from Labor Day to Memorial Day.

From the entrance, drive to the right past the first parking lot, to the beach area and its complex of modern buildings. The beach, food concessions, and rest rooms (open only in summer) make this a good place to end a walk.

TRAIL

After parking in one of the nearby lots, cross a bridge near the buildings, then begin the hike by following a walkway of fine gravel around to the right. You'll be passing an open field to the right and large trees along the shoreline to the left.

In minutes you will be on a paved road at the water's edge and climbing one of the many inclines on this route. The road alternately goes down to the very edge of the pond, then climbs many feet above it. In all seasons but summer you can see the water through the trees virtually throughout the walk. The pond is the star of this show, its rocky shoreline, wooded islands, and numerous coves all pleasing to the eyes in every season.

At a gravel roadway to the left, leading to a boat ramp, you'll have gone about 0.7 mile. Just beyond, the paved road climbs another hill and curls away from the pond briefly. Just off the road, to the right, is a string of houses, a reminder of just how close this park lies to residential areas.

When the road drops downhill again, you will reach a concrete wall and small dam, invariably crowded with people fishing. This is approximately the halfway point of the walk. Just beyond the dam you can leave the pavement, swinging left into the woods. There are numerous paths here, but there is little chance of getting lost. The pond is on one side and the road on the other. The best rule is to follow the shore.

You will reach a spot where it seems there are two ponds separated by a narrow strip of land. This is actually a dead-end point; stay to the right and resume walking the shoreline. There are huge, jagged boulders that might make you forget you're in such a "city park"— unless you can smell hot dogs being grilled at the picnic tables along the road.

The path snakes between the boulders and emerges onto the road almost directly across from a very small pond. Turn left and follow the road a short distance until it curves right. You can go left through a

Walking the roadways at Lincoln Woods has long been a family affair.

143

picnic area beside inviting rocks that offer lovely views of the lake. Again, you can follow the shoreline, but in 100 yards or so you will reach a boggy area that will require a right turn through the woods and out to the road.

You will soon pass the entrance road on your right and then a fishing access road on your left. Remain on the main park road until you reach a parking area in a grove of tall pines.

Walk along the rear of the parking lot, then cut across a grassy slope where there are many picnic tables and a rest room. Take a few moments to look over an ancient cemetery surrounded by a thick stone wall. This is the resting place of the Olney family, for whom the pond was named. Some of the tombstones date from the 1700s.

Walk down the slope to the water's edge, then follow a wide path to the right. It will take you around the final corner of the pond to the beach. Your walk will be finished, and it will be time for a plunge or a picnic.

32. Dame Farm–Snake Den

One walk back in time to view a vanishing life-style and another to see rattlesnake dens

Hiking distance: 3½ miles
Hiking time: 2½ hours

These two walks, almost in the shadow of Providence and the metropolitan population, remain among the farthest removed in feeling and tempo. Snake Den State Park and its featured attraction, Dame Farm, lie within a few miles of thousands of people, yet they belong to another era, a simpler time when each family formed its own community. The Dame Farm walk, in particular, gives you a look back at Rhode Island farming, a vanishing life-style.

I split these walks into separate strolls, but they could be walked together if you don't mind walking some distance on a paved road. Together they total slightly more than 3½ miles. Walking them separately still involves some road walking as well as the moving of your car. The individual walks total about 3 miles.

Of the two, the Dame Farm walk is easily the more popular, although some of the former highlights have changed or vanished in recent years. You still are able to get a good look at a working farm and can visit its fields and woodlots, but a landmark tree went down in 1991 and some of the interpretive signs along a woods path are no longer in place.

The second trail is, for the most part, simply a pleasant forest walk, but it takes you among the rugged rock ledges where the famed rattlesnakes, for which Snake Den Park was named, supposedly lived. I recommend you take your time walking the farm paths first, then if you still have ambition, visit the ledge area. The best ledges are near Brown Avenue, where you will be parking, so you can either take a look at the ledges and return to your car or walk the entire Snake Den circuit described here.

ACCESS

To reach the park, which stretches along the east side of Brown Avenue in Johnston, follow US 6 west 2 miles from I-295 and turn right onto Brown Avenue. You will reach Dame Farm, on the right, in 1.6 miles. From northern Rhode Island, take RI 5 south 1 mile from the US 44/RI 5 junction in Greenville, then turn right onto Brown Avenue. The farm is 1½ miles on the left.

Use the visitors' parking lot beside a produce stand near the road. To begin this hike, walk to the barn, which is listed in the National Registry of Historic Places. Your walk will start on a farm lane that runs to the left of the barn.

TRAIL

Just after you begin walking the lane, you'll see a small family cemetery in a field on the left. It's worth the short walk to it, but

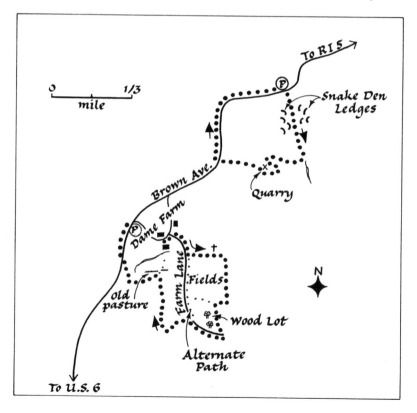

Visitors to Dame Farm get to look at a working farm as well as roaming woodland trails.

remember that this is a working farm—the livelihood of the Dame family—so if you visit during growing season and the field is planted in corn or wheat, it might be prudent to skip the graveyard until another time.

Even if you visit the graveyard, return to the lane to resume your tour. Follow the lane until you reach the first of two tiny ponds, then take a tractor trail that runs to the left just before the first pond. This lane will take you to a field that is bordered on the far side by woods. At the corner of this narrow field, look for a path that runs to the right through the woodlot.

You will emerge in a few minutes into another field that for decades was the Dame family's apple orchard. Many of the trees went down during the 1938 hurricane and the years took their toll on nearly all the others.

Walk to the right along the field edge and you will reach the last few apple trees. At this point you will rejoin the farm lane you were on earlier when you left the barn. Look back at the farm buildings. I like this rear view of the farm; having the fields stretch out in front of you with the proud old barn and silo as the backdrop makes for an idyllic scene indeed.

You could follow the lane right back to the barn, but to see more of the forest, look for a path that cuts off to the left just as the lane makes a curve to the right (this will be before you pass the ponds). For many years this path into the woods was marked by signs that detailed past uses of the area and the transition that took place as open fields were abandoned and the forest changed. Now, many of the signs are gone and some of those still standing are outdated, perhaps underlining how constantly and rapidly these changes occur.

This trail was originally easy to follow, but some recent growth along the route and the fading of the white blazes mean more care must be taken to avoid wandering off. The trail curves back toward the buildings, but at one point a side path cuts to the left, crosses a low ridge, and joins an old woods lane. If you find yourself on this lane, simply take it to the right. It will take you to a barbed wire fence just a few steps from where you should be. Follow the fence to the right.

The correct trail runs through a boulder field before reaching and passing through an opening in the barbed wire fence. In the past the trail emerged onto a hillside pasture that offered a panoramic view of the farm buildings and fields below. The pasture's focal point was a magnificent oak tree well over 200 years old. Now, however, the tree's huge stump is hidden by surging saplings and bushes, and you have to walk some distance down the slope to get good views of the farm.

You can end the walk by strolling down to the barn; but if you want more walking, look for a faint lane along the left side of this overgrown pasture, and take it back uphill into the woods. A path runs off this lane, to the right, and passes through an opening in a stone wall. This path curls through a pretty section of forest and crosses small brooks before it runs out onto Brown Avenue. Simply follow the curving road, to the right, back to your car.

If you want to see the snake dens of Snake Den Park, check your odometer and drive exactly 1 mile northeast on Brown Avenue. Park at a spot where there is a wide shoulder on the left and a dirt lane going into the forest on the right. (You will pass two other dirt trails before reaching this one. If you are unsure which lane is correct, drive out to RI 5 and return. The lane will be ½ mile from the highway.)

It's a short walk to the ledges that loom above the lane on both sides. There hasn't been a rattlesnake here in many years, but according to the old tales, they once were so thick that they kept horses and wagons from traveling on the old road.

Beyond the ledges the lane narrows and runs straight ahead. After passing through a second ravine, you'll reach a fork. The main trail goes on to a power line and leaves state property, so take the right fork. In minutes you'll emerge into an open area from which you can see houses along Brown Avenue. Go along the woods edge to the left, and in a few steps you'll find a trail returning to the forest.

This path circles around an abandoned stone quarry, which still has many stone slabs of interesting shapes, then runs downhill and out to Brown Avenue. Dame Farm will be 0.4 mile to your left; your car will be 0.6 mile to your right.

33. Osamequin Park

A leisurely stroll through a bird sanctuary

Hiking distance: 1 mile
Hiking time: 1 hour

O samequin Park is a tiny wildlife sanctuary that offers a leisurely stroll in a part of the state better known for congested traffic, mushrooming development, and all the other maladies of urban sprawl. This is a short walk—1 mile by the route described here—and made-to-order for those more interested in birds and plants than in chalking up miles.

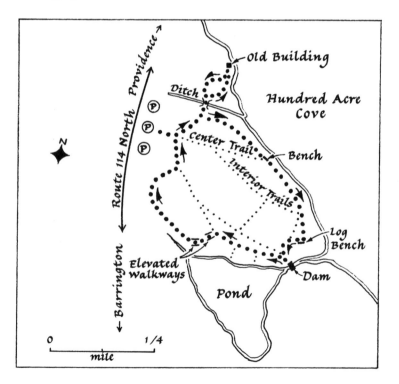

The walk's primary attraction is the wide, marshy segment of the Barrington River known as Hundred Acre Cove that forms the eastern boundary of the park. The sanctuary also includes a brackish pond, wetlands, several thickets, and some open meadows. All are filled with birds.

Osamequin Park, named for an American Indian chief who sold land in the area to colonists in 1653, is owned by the town of Barrington and maintained by the town and the Barrington Garden Club. A separate and smaller segment of the park lies about ½ mile farther north of the main sanctuary.

ACCESS

Osamequin Park is on RI 114 north, better known as the Wampanoag Trail, at the northern end of Barrington. Drivers coming from the north (Providence and East Providence) should look for the Zion Bible Institute exit on the right, then take the next opportunity to switch to the northbound lane of the divided highway. Those coming from the south should travel through Barrington center and watch for the park about a mile beyond the White Church, a local landmark. Signs for the refuge and a parking lot are just off the right shoulder of RI 114 north.

TRAIL

Walkers have a choice of routes because numerous trails run through the 42-acre sanctuary. Many visitors take a wide grassy path from the entrance directly across the park to a wooden bench beside the river. It's an excellent spot for checking on water birds.

However, to get the most out of a visit to Osamequin, I suggest making a circular walk that provides access to all of its various terrains and attractions. This route roughly follows the perimeter of the park and offers numerous vantage points near the water.

A word of caution: While the trails are kept open and clean, they are not well marked in some areas, and a new visitor can be confused by the many intersections. Trails are supposed to be marked in red, blue, yellow, and green, but the blazes are on posts instead of painted on trees and a number of posts are missing. Still, getting lost is not a worry in such a small park.

Just a few yards beyond the entrance is the first trail junction, at a bench and a sign in several languages. Go left on a path that curls through a wooded area, over a wooden walkway, and then across a

Idyllic Hundred Acre Cove draws walkers to Osamequin Park.

footbridge. Below the bridge is a ditch cut back in the 1930s in a mosquito-control project. Its water level rises and drops with the tide.

Beyond the bridge the path forks. Go right, and in a few minutes you will be at the river's edge. Chances are there will be egrets, swans, and other birds in the water at any time of year, and the place is often crowded with ducks and geese during spring and fall migrations.

Follow the shore until you reach a small, abandoned cement block building. In this area you may see people as well as birds wading in the shallow water, searching for shellfish. The clammers come here via a narrow path that runs from a small parking area along the highway.

Start retracing your steps along the shore, then go right at a fork that will take you into a thicket. This is a short trail that ends at the bridge you crossed earlier, but it may enable you to see woods birds you might otherwise miss.

After recrossing the bridge and the low walkway, turn left immediately. This path returns you to the river and takes you along the most popular and most picturesque section of the park. In front of you is the cove a park pamphlet called "Rhode Island's most extensive and pristine inland estuarine system." Beyond the marsh area you can see boats and homes. To the right is open water and the White Church on the horizon. Even without birds, it's easy to understand why people linger here.

When you are ready to resume walking, continue following the shoreline path until it ends at a log bench. Then go inland a few steps to an intersection, turn left, then take another left at the next fork, a four-trail junction. The left fork leads to a dam between the cove and a pond. A narrow trail to the right will provide your first look at the pond, which usually holds an abundance of herons, egrets, sandpipers, and other birds, along with muskrats, frogs, and turtles.

Return to the four-trail corner and go left. There are more markers, and you will be following the red trail as it weaves through dense thickets along the pond. Several side trails run to the water, although mud and tall reeds sometimes make viewing difficult.

When you reach an elevated walkway, cross it, and then take another walkway that goes through a junglelike growth of the reeds called phragmites. If you go when the reeds are not at full growth, or if you're tall, you can see most of the pond from the walkway.

By this time you will be back near the highway, and a short walk beyond the walkway will take you to the center trail. At this point, you can return to the parking lot and your car or take one of the interior trails for more birding.

34. Prudence Island South

Ferry ride and a walk in an island park through the densest deer population in Rhode Island

Hiking distance: 9 miles
Hiking time: 4–4½ hours

S olitude is an overriding theme on Prudence Island. A walk here offers plenty of ocean views, wildlife, and bits of history, both military and agricultural, but one of the best aspects is that crowds have not yet discovered this place.

Prudence Island lies virtually in the center of Narragansett Bay, and both ends of the island are state-owned and open to the public. Without restaurants and hotels on the island, however, Prudence does not attract the casual tourists in the manner of, say, a Block Island.

There have been changes on the island in recent years, and more changes are planned. For a time Prudence was considered the crown jewel of the Bay Islands Park System, and boats brought day trippers to the parks at both ends of the island. Also, a small campground flourished at South Prudence State Park. Then the trips were stopped and the campground closed, partly because of problems with deer ticks, which can transmit Lyme disease. The miles of lanes and old roads were virtually unused for a few years.

Now Prudence seems to be entering still another era. The state and a local group called the Prudence Conservancy have purchased more property, and the island has become the Narragansett Bay National Estuarine Research Reserve. At present, few of the plans for new trails and other amenities have taken shape, but the features that have long made Prudence a special place to the outdoors-minded—deer, songbirds, waterfowl, flowers—are still readily available, along with the history of the place and the views of the bay.

This 9-mile walk (which is also a good bike ride) goes from the ferry landing in Homestead, around the south end of the island, past old military bunkers, back up through the middle of the island on a woods lane, and then past a vineyard before returning to Homestead. (For a description of a walk through North Prudence Park see Walk 16 in *More Walks & Rambles in Rhode Island*, Backcountry Publications.)

All but 1 mile of this walk is on gravel and concrete roads, and staying on these roads lessens your chances of coming in contact with deer ticks. Going in winter, late fall, or early spring will also help avoid the ticks.

ACCESS

The ferry to Homestead runs from Bristol on the east side of Narragansett Bay, with a couple of daily trips each way in summer and fewer in other seasons. Schedules change frequently, so it is best to check ahead by calling the Prudence Island Navigation Company. The departure point in Bristol is on Thames Street at the foot of Church Street.

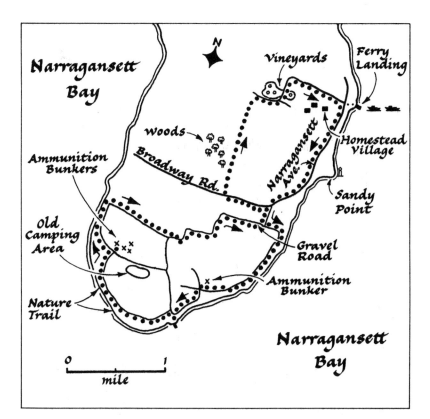

TRAIL

From the landing in Homestead, go left on the first street, Narragansett Avenue, which follows the shoreline past Sandy Point, a dock area that features a small lighthouse. There are often small boats moored here, and flocks of cormorants, gulls, terns, and other water birds are not uncommon.

Follow the road as it runs uphill, away from the water and out of the village. Pass the island's fire department garage, then, where the main road makes a sharp right turn, go straight ahead on a secondary road. This road ends quickly at a T intersection. The road to the right is the entrance to state property, and you will return on this road, but for now turn left, pass a barway, and take a narrow lane down toward the water.

Hidden in vines and brush to the left of this lane is a high fence topped with barbed wire. This fence, put up back when the navy considered Prudence one of the key points in its defense plans for Narragansett Bay in World War II, still zigzags across most of the island. For years the fence marked the boundary of the state's property on this end of the island.

The gravel lane turns to the right at the water and follows the shoreline. Even though surging undergrowth blocks views of the water in many places, there are breaks through which you can see the barges, lobster boats, sailing vessels, and other craft that use the bay regularly. Across the East Passage you can see Mount Hope Bridge to the extreme left, some of the buildings of Portsmouth directly east, and the Newport Bridge to the extreme right.

Birds abound in this section, as the lane is lined with numerous bushes and vines that produce berries. You also are likely to see deer tracks here and perhaps the deer themselves as Prudence has a large deer population. Chances of seeing deer depend a great deal on the time of your visit, as well as luck and powers of observation. Mornings and evenings are better than midafternoon, and all other seasons are better than midsummer. Still, not long ago, on an afternoon walk in early August, I found a beautiful speckled fawn beside one of the roads.

The first sign of the old military activity—other than the barbed wire—is an unused concrete boat ramp you reach about 2½ miles from your start. Just beyond the ramp, the lane surface turns to concrete and you pass the first of the many underground ammunition bunkers that lie along your route. Closed and barred to the public, each shows only concrete fronts and a rounded top covered with grass and bushes.

At a crossroads, turn left toward the water, and follow this road as it runs along the shore to a long dock, now used mostly as a fishing pier by park visitors. You may be able to pick up a pamphlet there for a nature trail that begins at the dock. Most of the nature trail's numbered posts call attention to plants, but some also point out historical features or places visible across the water.

With or without a brochure, following the nature trail is worthwhile. From the dock, take the path as it goes left along the shore, passing a pole and platform put up for ospreys. In addition to the birds and plants close at hand, you have excellent views over the waves of Jamestown Island, Quonset Point (a former navy air station), and Hope Island as you make your way west and then north.

Where the lane intersects with a concrete road near another bunker, the nature trail and its posts turn to the right, going through what had been the campground. You could walk that way to see the park's interior, but a more picturesque route would be to remain on the gravel lane as it turns left and resumes its shoreline run. It stays at the water's edge for a short distance, then turns right and curls inland to a complex of buildings.

When you reach a large garage, take a paved road that runs behind the garage past several other buildings. The road will take you to the gravel lane that is the park's connector with the rest of the island. Follow this gravel road for more than 1 mile, until you reach the T junction you saw earlier. Go left and in moments you will be back on the island's main road, called Broadway in this area.

You will have walked roughly 7 miles by this point and could easily

Views of the bay and boats are among the attractions of Prudence Island.

retrace your steps back to the village. But doing so would cause you to miss a delightful segment, and perhaps your best chance of seeing deer. Instead, turn left on Broadway for 0.3 mile, until you reach a wooden fence on the right.

Behind the fence is a grassy lane that I consider one of the most pleasant segments of this entire walk. It runs for 1 mile through onetime farmland that has returned to forest. You will pass impressive stone walls, some of the island's tallest trees, and, after about ½ mile, an abandoned apple orchard that is ideal deer habitat. The open areas and the apples still on the old trees attract many deer, so walk quietly.

Eventually the lane ends at a gravel road, directly across from a house. Turn right on the road. You will soon be walking beside a high fence that protects a vineyard, no longer in business. Better views of the many rows of grape vines lie ahead, because at the first intersection you will turn left onto a road that runs between two vineyards.

Beyond the vineyards the road turns right and then becomes pavement as you reenter the village of Homestead. You'll soon be walking downhill, past houses, heading directly for the ferry landing.

35. Ruecker Wildlife Refuge

A short walk along the Sakonnet River to see fiddler crabs

Hiking distance: 1½ miles
Hiking time: 1½ hours

This walk is a little jewel. Looping through the Emilie Ruecker Wildlife Refuge, it is only 1½ miles long on an easy-to-walk path. If you like birds and fiddler crabs, you are likely to be fascinated every step of the way.

The refuge, located on the salty shores of the Sakonnet River in Tiverton, was a 30-acre farm before the owner, Emilie Ruecker, donated it to the Rhode Island Audubon Society in 1965. Now, thanks to its natural attributes—shallow marshes and upland woodlots—and Audubon management, the refuge attracts a wide variety of bird life, particularly during the spring and fall migrations. The fiddler crabs and some unusual rock formations add to the attraction, but for most walkers it is the birds that make the trails of Ruecker so inviting.

ACCESS

Follow RI 77 south from the village of Tiverton for 3 miles to Sapowet Road. Turn right and drive ½ mile to the refuge, which is on the right. The sign and small parking lot are inconspicuous, so look carefully.

TRAIL

As soon as you leave the car, you will start hearing birds. In spring and early summer quail whistle from the surrounding pastures and hay fields, and warblers and catbirds call from within the sanctuary's dense growth of bushes and small trees. In fall migrating swallows, sometimes in the thousands, gather in this area before heading south. In winter a feeding station near the entrance, operated by the Audubon people, draws chickadees, nuthatches, and nearly every other bird that

159

usually winters in the state. Over the course of a year, about 150 species of birds frequent the little refuge.

The trails are blazed in yellow, blue, and red, and a short side trail is marked in white. Even with frequent stops to observe the birds, you can easily walk all these trails in 1½ to 2 hours.

From the parking lot, take the yellow trail that starts beside a large wooden sign where trail maps are usually available. The trail runs through a small pine grove, and you'll quickly come to the white path, which goes left to an observation blind at a shallow pond. In most seasons you can find herons, egrets, ducks, and perhaps bitterns, sandpipers, and other birds here.

Beyond the pines you will enter the old farm fields, now overgrown with bushes, many of which produce berries that attract numerous birds. Catbirds are abundant here, along with mockingbirds, thrashers, orioles, thrushes, and goldfinches. Quail and pheas-

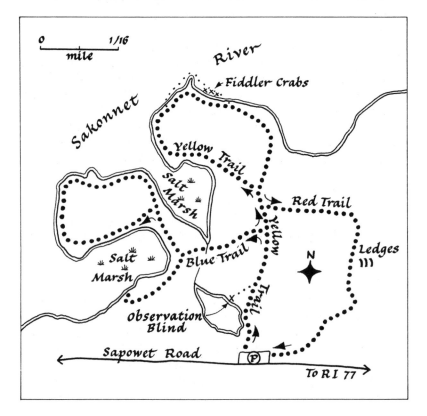

Salt marshes surround much of the Emilie Ruecker Wildlife Refuge.

ants reside in the areas that are kept relatively open.

You will quickly reach the blue-blazed trail, breaking off to the left. Follow it for your first look at the salt marshes. The first segment takes you through a dense thicket and over a narrow brook; then, when you reach the marsh, the trail forks. A side trail swings left, down to the edge of a small cove. During most of the year you can expect to see shorebirds feeding in the shallows, particularly herons and big, white American and snowy egrets that are familiar figures throughout the area.

The main trail loops around the perimeter of a small peninsula, offering good views of the marshes and river at several high points.

161

Dense shadbush and bayberry add color in early spring and attract even more birds (waxwings, titmice, cardinals) in summer.

When you return to the yellow trail, keep left for another circular walk on a higher peninsula. There you will find more evidence that this birdland was once farmland. Several stone walls mark off forgotten fields, and an overgrown but still visible tractor lane twice cuts across the footpath.

The trail clings to the very edge of this point of land, 8 to 10 feet above the water's surface. Although there are few tall trees, the undergrowth is extremely thick. Several openings do, however, provide good overlooks. When you notice the trail starting to curve back, take a side path down to the beach and the fiddler crabs. Walk the beach around the point for your best look at the tiny crabs, which are named for the one disproportionately large claw that resembles a base fiddle. Hundreds of tiny holes in the sand betray their presence, and on warm, sunny days you will be likely to see hundreds of them scurrying across the beach or hiding just inside their burrows. For many walkers, particularly those with small children, the fiddlers may be the highlight of Ruecker.

After you climb back up to the yellow trail, finish the loop until you reach the red-blazed path going off to the left. Turn and enter the deepest woods on the refuge. There still are few tall trees, but in these woods you will find some oaks and hickories and a stand of alders. Alders frequently mean woodcocks, because these small trees thrive in the same moist ground where the long-billed birds probe for earthworms.

The red trail winds along low but unusual rock ledges. Small pebbles appear to be cemented together; local residents call it pudding stone. This sedimentary bedrock, estimated to be 250 million years old, is found few other places than the Narragansett Bay basin. A similar, though larger, mass formed Hanging Rock in the Norman Bird Sanctuary (Walk 36).

These ledges do not extend far, however. The trail soon swings right through dense woods (great for warblers and flycatchers), crosses the faint tractor road once more, then emerges at the parking lot.

36. Norman Bird Sanctuary

The largest range of bird species and a visit to Hanging Rock

Hiking distance: 3½ miles
Hiking time: 2 hours

The Norman Bird Sanctuary, east of Newport, is unique among Rhode Island walking areas for several reasons. It is one of the few places that charges a fee for entering, but some of its other qualities can make you feel the place is well worth the cost.

Norman, a privately owned property, has a natural history museum. There are usually live hawks or owls or other birds on the premises recovering from injuries, and it is truly a sanctuary for birds of all kinds. You may see more species on these trails than on any other in this book. Rock hounds will love the place for its outstanding examples of conglomerate called pudding stone.

The trails wander back and forth over the refuge's 450-plus acres, and on the 3½-mile walk described here you will travel three parallel yet distinct ridges. One ridge leads to the famed Hanging Rock, from which you can see over Gardiner Pond and the ocean beach; another offers views of Grey Craig Pond, its waterfowl, and a mansion beyond. Other trails pass through forests and around swamps, and one runs through a wooded area managed for woodcocks.

ACCESS

To reach the sanctuary from the west side of Narragansett Bay, cross the Newport Bridge, take RI 138, and continue straight east, via Miantonomi Avenue and Green End Avenue, until you reach Third Beach Road. Go right (south) on Third Beach Road less than 1 mile. The refuge is on the right.

From the east side of the bay, drive RI 138 south to Mitchells Lane, turn left and go 2 miles to an intersection, then bear right onto Third

Beach Road. Norman is 1 mile farther on the right.

The sanctuary is closed on Mondays (except holidays). The admission fee covers use of the trails as well as access to the exhibits. Pick up a trail map, which provides information about side trails not included here.

TRAIL

The walk starts behind the refuge buildings. Trails here are seldom blazed in the usual manner—paint splotches on trees—but there are numerous signs to keep you from getting lost. Follow the main entrance path downhill, past the first signs and side trails, until you reach a bridge. This bridge is part of a dam and dike built to help regulate water in Red Maple Swamp, a great place to see waterfowl, just to the right.

Just beyond the bridge you will reach an intersection of several

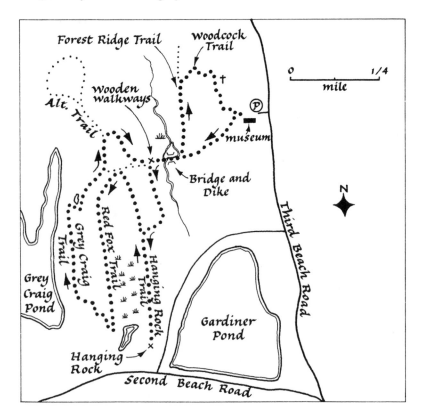

wooden walkways over boggy areas. Look for the sign pointing to Hanging Rock, to the left. The rocky ridge will be your next objective.

The trail goes through dense forest and soon takes you up the first ridge, which appears to be made up almost entirely of the fascinating pudding stone. This rock mass, formed eons ago, is composed of countless granite pebbles seemingly cemented together. Pudding stone, while relatively rare elsewhere, is common throughout the Narragansett Bay basin, but there may be no other place where it is as prominent as at Norman.

Once you climb the ridge, turn left toward Hanging Rock. For about ¼ mile you will walk above the surrounding trees. The walking is relatively easy, although the footing can be slippery when wet. The path ends abruptly at Hanging Rock, which seems to hang over the surrounding countryside. Pause a while and take in the views. Below, to the left, is Gardiner Pond, where geese and ducks often congregate in fall. Beyond the pond is the Sachuest Point National Wildlife Refuge (Walk 14, *More Walks & Rambles in Rhode Island*, Backcountry Publications) as well as the Atlantic ocean and a public beach. Ahead is Newport and its shoreline, plus the stone tower of St. George's School. Below, to the right, is a marshy area and, beyond, another rocky ridge.

When you are ready to resume walking, retrace your steps along the ridge, past the point where you climbed up. The trail follows the crest, then descends to a trail intersection. Turn left. In a few yards you will reach another junction with signs indicating Valley Trail (with dead-ends at the marsh you saw from Hanging Rock), Red Fox Trail, and Grey Craig Trail. Red Fox and Grey Craig start together, then quickly split. Take Red Fox to the left; you'll return on Grey Craig.

Red Fox Trail climbs the second ridge, which is about as high as the first ridge but not quite as exposed. Cedars and other small trees grow through the cracks, although most of the plant life is twisted by constant buffeting of the wind. I remember walking this trail in November one year, and it seemed every robin in Rhode Island had gathered here, feeding on cedar berries, before heading south. Cedar waxwings, catbirds, kingbirds, and various sparrows and warblers often dally in this area too.

You'll also see a low stone wall wandering along the ridge, sometimes on one side, sometimes on the other. The top of a narrow rock ridge seems a strange place for such a wall.

When you reach the end of the ridge, the path curls down to the

Wooden walkways provide easy access to some areas of the Norman Bird Sanctuary.

right. It then narrows considerably as it crosses a tiny valley, via a walkway, and climbs the third ridge.

You will be on Grey Craig Trail, heading back toward the interior of the refuge. To the left is Grey Craig Pond, and there are some good overlooks. The best viewing spots, however, are farther down the trail, after it runs through woods briefly and then returns to a rocky summit above the shallower backwaters of the pond. During migration you will likely see geese, ducks, and perhaps loons and other waterfowl here. Some ducks remain throughout the summer, when you also should see swans and shorebirds of several kinds. Across the water stands Grey Craig, an impressive mansion built in the 1920s. The outcroppings are good places to linger.

When the trail descends, it curls into the woods around a tiny pond—no more than a water hole—and returns to the Valley Trail junction you passed earlier. By this point you will have walked about 2½ miles, and you could return to your car by walking straight ahead and crossing the dike bridge. Grey Craig Trail, however, goes left, almost across from Valley Trail. Take the left trail. It provides another look at the sanctuary interior, along with access to the property's newest segment, if so desired. At the first fork you must make a decision. Taking the left fork would take you over a brook and into a hilly forest before bringing you back. It would extend the hike to about 4¼ miles instead of 3½. If you take the right fork, you'll be back to the dike quickly.

After crossing the bridge once more, you could simply go back uphill to the buildings and your car, but I recommend turning left onto a wide path called Forest Ridge Trail. It runs through open, pleasant woods with numerous stone walls and boulders. Pass up the first major trail to the right, but take the second, Woodcock Trail, for the walk through an overgrown field. The first time I walked through here, I nearly stepped on a woodcock that had been probing for worms on the path. I haven't seen one here since, but I keep looking.

The trail ends at a small family graveyard. Turn right, following a lane along the sanctuary gardens, and in minutes you will be back at the refuge headquarters.

37. Cliff Walk

A walk along the Newport shoreline bluff for ocean views and marvelous mansions

Hiking distance: 6½ miles
Hiking time: 3 hours

Sooner or later, every Rhode Island walker has to try Cliff Walk. It is the state's most famous and most walked trail, a 3¼-mile walkway that follows the Newport shoreline. For the entire distance you have the sea on one side and magnificent mansions of another time on the other.

In summer this is a crowded walk, with numerous out-of-state tourists using it to get a free look at the mansions, among the most lavish homes ever built in America. The trail runs behind dozens of these 60- to 70-room "summer cottages" built in the late 1800s when Newport was the playground of the Vanderbilts and Astors, the Whartons and Belmonts, and other leaders of finance. Many of these mansions, which face Bellevue Avenue, are now open in the summer months as museumlike relics of a gilt-edged era.

A crisp spring or autumn day might be best for this walk, because not only is the trail crowded in summer but heat tends to smudge the sea views. There is virtually no shade for the entire distance, and most of the walkway is concrete or gravel, so a beating sun can make the hiking too hot for you to get the most out of it.

ACCESS

To reach Cliff Walk's start, take RI 138 into Newport, turn south on RI 138A or RI 214, and continue to Memorial Boulevard. Turn right and you will quickly reach the state-owned Easton Beach, where you can park. There is room for several cars on the street. Parking is limited to 3 hours, but you can walk the entire Cliff Walk and return in that time. The beach parking lot carries a fee in summer but is free the rest of the year.

If you wish to make a one-way walk, you can park another car on

168

Ledge Road or Ocean Avenue near Cliff Walk's end. Take Memorial Boulevard to Bellevue Avenue, turn left, and drive past the mansions. Ledge Road is a narrow street that runs to Land's End, where many walkers conclude their trek. There is no parking allowed at the end of the street, but there is room for a few cars farther up. Some visitors walk to privately owned Bailey Beach on Ocean Avenue, a short distance beyond Land's End, but there also is limited parking at that site.

A simple solution might be to just walk back to Easton Beach. If backtracking along Cliff Walk is undesirable, simply go out Ledge Road and turn right on Bellevue Avenue. This way you can see the front of some of the mansions as well as those on the opposite side of the street. Bellevue Avenue is shaded with immense beech trees and can be one of the most pleasant city strolls anywhere, eventually running by a shopping area and the famed Tennis Casino before reaching Memorial Boulevard. By street, the return is just over 3 miles,

making a round-trip of about 6½ miles, rather easily done in 3 hours.

TRAIL

Starting at Easton Beach, walk uphill to Cliff Walk's start, just behind a restaurant called Cliff Walk Manor. You will quickly rise high above the sea. The path is a sidewalk that twists and turns as it follows the shore. For the most part, fences or hedges, or both, line the right side. On the left is open ocean. To the far left, across a cove, you can see Middletown, Easton Point, and Sachuest Point.

In a matter of minutes you will reach Forty Steps, originally a natural rock formation leading down to the water but now a concrete stairway and observation platform. Just beyond, the walkway was recently repaired with new retaining walls below the path. Erosion and constant battering by waves require frequent work on the path, and occasionally sections are closed to the public for brief periods. In such cases, detour routes on city streets are devised.

Beyond the first area, where you can see large buildings now part of Salve Regina University, you will reach a permanently open iron gate. This is Cliff Walk's "entrance" to The Breakers, the Italian-style palace Cornelius Vanderbilt commissioned in 1895. A rose hedge, a wrought-iron fence, and a vast lawn separate the trail from the mansion, but several breaks in the hedge enable you to marvel at the awesome size of the 70-room "cottage."

The rugged shoreline draws walkers to Newport's Cliff Walk.

For the length of Cliff Walk, the pounding sea is on one side and the opulent mansions of another era are on the other.

After passing a second iron gate and several more immense homes, the trail turns and climbs a few steps between cement and brick walls. Behind a high white wall on the right is Rosecliff, the famed mansion used in filming the movie *The Great Gatsby*. Unfortunately, not much of the building can be seen from Cliff Walk.

Ahead loom some of the walk's better-known features, including a Chinese-style teahouse almost directly above the trail. This was Mrs. Otto Belmont's tearoom when she resided at Marble House. You will pass through a curving tunnel nearly beneath the pagoda, then swing left and pass through another short tunnel through a rocky ridge called Sheep Point.

You will then leave sidewalks behind for good. The path is gravel and dirt in some places, large rocks in others. It swings around the aptly named Rough Point, where surf often sprays high after crashing onto the boulders below. Throughout this area the trail can be hazardous, particularly when wet, so use care.

At Rough Point you will cross a deep chasm on a wooden bridge, then cover another 100 yards or so of rough footing before the path goes up and follows the edge of a fenced lawn. This area provides excellent views of several more huge homes built in European style.

When the trail breaks out onto a street, you will be facing the last mansion on the route, Land's End, once the George Eustis Paine estate. The street is Ledge Road, and you will turn right to reach your car or to walk back to Easton Beach. A path around the stone mansion would take you to Bailey Beach and Ocean Avenue.

171

38. Beavertail Park

An island walk through military and sailing history

Hiking distance: 3 miles
Hiking time: 2 hours

A walk in Beavertail State Park is one that can be fascinating at any time of year. And you don't have to wait for good weather. In fact, in many ways it is more alluring, more inspiring, in stormy weather.

Beavertail is located at the southern tip of Jamestown Island in

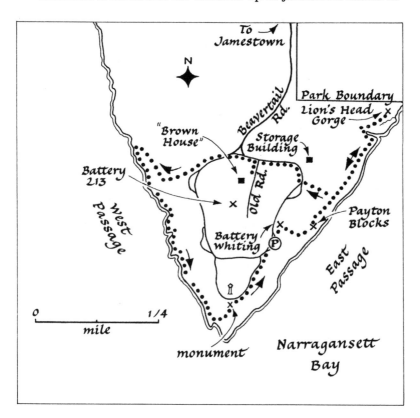

Narragansett Bay. It is part of Rhode Island's new Bay Islands Park System and is still in the early stages of development. There are no marked hiking trails at the present, but a scenic and most interesting walk of about 3 miles can be made by following the rocky shoreline and cutting across the center of the park, while checking out numerous bits of military and sailing history.

ACCESS

Reaching the park is not difficult; only one road—Beavertail Road—runs due south out of the village of Jamestown. Follow it into the park, continue past the first few parking areas, swing around the lighthouse, and park in the first lot just beyond. Here, overlooking the pounding surf, is the ideal place to begin and end your visit.

Once, this point was among the most notorious places in New England for sailors. Shipwrecks dot its history—more than 30 vessels have been destroyed or run aground here in the past 150 years—and when the waves are high and they crash onto the rocks below, it's easy to imagine how treacherous this place can be in a storm. In fact, you can still find a bit of cargo from a ship that went down in 1859.

In calmer weather this is a place of beauty. Photographers and artists often can be found here, recording the white spray of the surf gleaming in the sunshine. Other visitors simply sit on the rocks and drink in the scenery.

TRAIL

You can walk either direction, but for this stroll, go left (east). A narrow path runs from the parking lot into a thicket of bushes. In a few steps you'll find the concrete facing of Battery Whiting, one of the bunkers established on Beavertail to protect Narragansett Bay during World War II. The bunker itself has now been sealed off, but a few more steps to the left will take you to an observation station, which you can walk into. Gun placements just outside the station guarded the bay's East Passage.

After looking over these remnants of what was Fort Burnside, return to the parking lot, follow a path down to the shoreline rocks, and head east. In the distance, across the water, you can see Newport. The nimble can walk on the large but uneven rocks. There also is a faint path farther up the shore, where the grass meets the rocks. In this area look for rectangular granite blocks among the rocks; these were destined for Alexandria, Virginia, aboard the *H.F. Payton* when it sank here well over a century ago after crashing into Shipwreck Rock. The building blocks rested beneath the waves until the hurricane of 1938 flung about a dozen of them onto the rocks. On close inspection you can see the flowery designs chiseled into the granite.

Throughout this section there are good views, looking back, of the lighthouse. Many seabirds frequent this area—terns, cormorants, and gulls in summer; scoters, eiders, and mergansers in winter.

Continue along the rocks for some distance, until you reach a deep chasm that cannot be crossed on rocks. This is Lion's Head Gorge. You can take a path up into the bushes and around the chasm a few more yards to see how the place got its name. At a point from which you can see Newport Bridge, there is a jagged cleft in the rocks into which the tide flows, often resulting in a loud crashing sound that reminded an early visitor of a lion's roar.

The path goes on beyond this point, but you would soon be leaving state property; so after looking over the chasm, return along the rocky shore, toward the lighthouse, until you reach a concrete headwall. A path around the wall leads to a parking lot (not the lot where you began). Turn right onto the paved road and follow it as it circles inland. You will pass, on your left, a brown building with high radio antennae and, on your right, a metal, round-top storage building.

There are few places better for experiencing the waves of lower Narragansett Bay than the rocks of Beavertail Park.

174

An abandoned roadway runs toward the brown building, which looks like a house but was a special wartime structure built as an identification and communications center to monitor all incoming vessels. Great pains were taken to make the building resemble a summer cottage, but the walls are three feet thick, some of the "windows" were merely painted decorations, and the real windows were equipped with metal shields. The building is now a caretaker's home and is off-limits to visitors.

Also near the abandoned road, between the brown building and the lighthouse, hidden in a tangle of tall bushes, is Battery 213, an underground complex used by the navy during the war. During the summer months a park naturalist conducts tours of the bunker, but visitors are advised not to attempt exploration on their own. The complex is in total darkness and holes in the floors make wandering around extremely dangerous.

Stay on the park road as it loops through the park interior. Pass the exit road and cross the road on which you entered. Beyond it, behind a stop sign, pick up a faint lane that runs toward the ocean. It will run parallel to the shore for a while, then you'll see a cutoff path to the cliffs. Turn left at the cliffs on the narrow footpath that runs above the water's edge.

For the rest of the way you will be following this path back toward the lighthouse. Much of the time the path is at the very edge of cliffs above the jagged rocks, and you will have to make like a mountain goat in clinging to the trail. For the less agile there are other paths farther back in the bushes, but they offer less of a challenge and do not permit as many good views of the surf.

This side of Beavertail usually is more sheltered than the southern and eastern exposures, particularly in winter, and as such is a favorite place for birders, many of whom use the parking facilities just above. During stormy weather, flocks of brant, scaup, and other wintering ducks and geese rest on this side, and rare birds frequently seek refuge near this cliff. In summer sandpipers feed on the rocks, and there are always terns soaring by.

In the thick bushes above the water, numerous songbirds that usually migrate south—meadowlarks, robins, flickers, various sparrows—linger throughout the winter. You also are likely to see several species of hawks here.

Once you pass a tall wooden post, just as the lighthouse comes into view, the walking becomes easier, although you still have to swing inland around chasms a few times. You can climb down onto the rocks at several places, giving you a chance to look over the barnacles and other marine life found there and perhaps feel the salt spray. Below the lighthouse you will cross one area covered with small, blue clamshells.

Climb back up to the road when you see a large foghorn installed beside a stone monument. The inscription notes that the spot is the site of Beavertail's first lighthouse, built in 1749, the third to be established on the Atlantic coast. Your car will be a short distance to the right, but before leaving take another look at the timeless ocean; it hasn't changed in all these years, yet it is never exactly the same on any two visits.

39. Block Island South

A visit to the famous Mohegan Bluffs on the southern end of historic Block Island

Hiking distance: 8½ miles
Hiking time: 3½–4 hours

I f you are looking for something unique in your walk, take a trip to Block Island. There you can walk for many miles and continue to see sights not available anywhere else in Rhode Island.

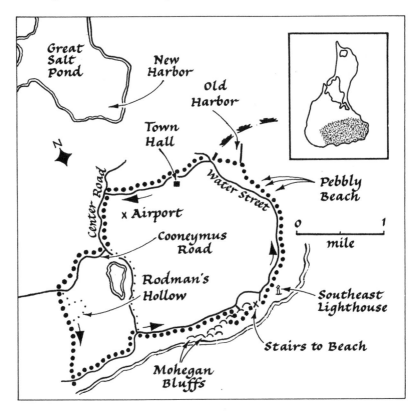

Block Island, 12 miles south of Rhode Island's mainland, once was a farming and fishing community. Later it became something of a resort and vacation spot, earning the nickname "Bermuda of the North." The beaches and shops and restaurants still draw crowds in summer, but in autumn—the best time to visit the island—the place is still a wonderland of seascapes, cliffs, plant life, bird life, and history.

The walk described here—8½ miles through the central and southeastern regions of the island, visiting the spectacular Mohegan Bluffs—is one of the more popular routes, although far more visitors use mopeds and bicycles than their feet. Except for the mile walk through an intriguing place called Rodman's Hollow, the distance is easily enough traveled on wheels, but I always have the feeling even mopeds and bikes are too fast; their riders miss too much.

ACCESS

As with our other Block Island hike (Walk 40), this one begins and ends in the village of New Shoreham at Old Harbor, where the ferry boats from Point Judith and Providence drop off and pick up passengers. The walk takes 3½ to 4 hours, so it may be best to take the Point Judith ferry, which takes only about an hour to reach the island. It leaves from a state pier in the village of Galilee. The Providence boat ride, which includes a stop in Newport, takes about three hours, which would not leave much time for walking if you plan to return the same day.

Schedules vary with the season, and sometimes change within a season, so check departure times in advance. The ferry makes several round-trip runs each day during the summer, two daily in spring and fall, and just one a day in winter.

TRAIL

From the landing, turn right on the first street (Water Street), and go past the souvenir shops and the first of the large wooden hotels that were built when New Shoreham was in its heyday at the turn of the century. Turn left on Chapel Street (between the Harborside Inn and the New Shoreham House) and start uphill into the residential area. Shortly, Chapel Street merges with Old Town Road. You will pass the town hall and quickly reach the island's interior.

If you are used to forest walks, you will be struck by the absence of tall trees. Early settlers cut the trees while carving out their farms, and ocean winds that buffet the island, frequently mercilessly in winter, prevent new vegetation from gaining much height.

Still, there is much greenery all around. Old fruit trees (apples, pears, peaches) line the first section of Old Town Road, and many are now being engulfed by swarming grape vines. Bayberry bushes, blackberry and honeysuckle vines, sumac, and wild roses form thickets—virtually impenetrable walls—along the roadway. Wildflowers are common and colorful.

When you reach Center Road, about 1 mile from your start and marked by millstones set in the ground, turn left and climb a rather steep hill. The road swings to the right around the island airport. On the opposite side of the road, to your right, you will have an open view across lowlands to houses perched on hilltops along the western edge of the island.

At the next intersection, go right on Cooneymus Road. The first house on Cooneymus, on the left, is called "Smilin' Through," for it was here that Arthur Penn composed the hit song of that name in the 1920s. Trustom Dodge, one of the original island settlers, also had a home at this site in the 1600s.

After Cooneymus makes a sweeping curve to the left, you will come upon a wooden turnstile set in a stone wall on the left. A path running from the turnstile leads to a stone-walled rectangle that once contained a cemetery for some early island residents. Later, the spot became known for the single headstone that stood inside the walls, a stone inscribed "Dearly Beloved, Dinkle Mazzur" (Dinkle was a pet dog). That stone, too, has since been moved.

Shortly after the road curves right, you will reach Rodman's Hollow (look for a sign on the left). The hollow is supposedly one of the favorite haunts of the Block Island meadow vole, a mouselike animal found nowhere else on earth except this island. Hawks that feed on the vole and other small prey also are common in the hollow, along with numerous songbirds, especially during migration seasons.

Narrow paths drop down into the deep hollow from behind the wooden sign, but not only are they often overgrown with briars and poison ivy, they can be extremely confusing to first-time visitors. I recommend staying on Cooneymus Road beyond the Rodman's Hollow sign a short distance until reaching a dirt road going to the left.

This lane is Black Rock Road, one of my favorite walking places on the entire island. Off-limits to mopeds, it runs for about 1 mile, skirting the hollow and providing access to some of the better trails in the hollow. You can usually see hawks and often deer, or at the very least, deer tracks from this lane.

Southeast Lighthouse atop Mohegan Bluffs is a must for visitors to Block Island.

Shortly after entering Black Rock Road, you'll pass a path on the right and a sign for the Block Island Greenway (Walk 21, *More Walks & Rambles in Rhode Island*, Backcountry Publications), a trail that runs down the center of the island. Ignore this path, but a short distance beyond, you'll see a barway on the left and another Greenway sign. This is a good place to detour into the hollow for a closer look at the plants, birds, and butterflies. Since the trails in the hollow wander erratically, *take all right turns*. When you pass benches installed on a hillside, look for a narrow side path to the right. It will lead you back out to Black Rock Road.

As you near the shoreline, you will reach a junction with another dirt road, running left. This will be your way back to pavement, but first go a few yards straight ahead to the cliff above Black Rock beach. You can pause there and enjoy the sounds and sights of the surf far below, or you can take a path down to the water. This is roughly the halfway point in your walk, and it is a delightful place for a rest.

When you are ready to resume, return to the dirt road you passed just before the bluff (it will be on your right). It will take you past several homes and to some impressive overlooks before you reach pavement. Turn right on the paved road—Mohegan Trail—which runs to the island's most famous cliffs.

The bluffs were named for the Mohegan war party that was driven over these cliffs by the island's Indians, the Manisseans, in 1590. The bluffs tower 160 feet above the beach and ocean, and you can reach these cliffs by two chief cutoffs. I like to take the first side trail, an unmarked sandy lane that runs through the dunes from a point where the paved road jogs left. The lane runs to the edge of a cliff that provides spectacular views of bluffs on both sides as well as the Southeast Lighthouse in the distance on the left.

From this cliff, you can take a rather steep path to the right down to the beach. Be careful—it's a little treacherous.

Once on the beach, turn left and walk the few hundred yards to a wooden stairway. The 160 steps will take you back up the cliff to an observation platform. This spot is the most commonly used vista for both Mohegan Bluffs and Southeast Lighthouse.

When you return to the paved road, turn right. Ahead looms Southeast Lighthouse, which carries a beam ships can see for 30 miles. Near the lighthouse is a stone that lists the names of 16 ships that were wrecked along this shore, a list that ends with the chilling suffix "etc."

You will be on Southeast Light Road, heading back toward the village. The road name soon changes to Spring Street. Where the road runs near the water, you may want to leave the pavement one last time. You can cross the guardrail and take a path down the aptly named Pebbly Beach. It's just a short walk on this beach to an inn, an excellent place to refresh yourself while awaiting your ferry back to the mainland.

40. Block Island North

A varied walk along the more peaceful side of historic Block Island—a special place for rare bird sightings

Hiking distance: 9½ miles
Hiking time: 4–4½ hours

The northern end of Block Island offers the walker a wide variety of sights: a flotilla of boats and a lovely, quiet pond; a sand dune wildlife sanctuary and a dense, junglelike thicket; a low-lying spit of land and high cliffs.

This walk also offers less crowded areas than most of the island, which attracts increasingly large numbers of visitors and vacationers in summer. It is a long walk, well over 9 miles if you spend much time rambling in the thicket called The Maze, but it is an easy stroll, and, except for The Maze, nearly all of it is on one paved road.

As with the Block Island South hike (Walk 39), this route begins and ends at the ferry landing at Old Harbor in New Shoreham. This walk, however, is not a loop but a simple return on the same road, since there is only one road that runs to the northern tip, the place where white settlers first arrived on the island.

ACCESS

This walk takes approximately 4 hours, so it may be best to take the Point Judith ferry, which actually leaves from a state pier in the village of Galilee. The 12-mile trip takes only about one hour each way, as opposed to the three-hour ride on the ferry from Providence. Six hours on the ferry would not leave much time for walking if you intend to spend only one day.

Schedules vary with the season and sometimes change within a season, so check departure times in advance. The ferry makes several round-trip runs each day during the summer, two daily in spring and fall, and just one a day in winter.

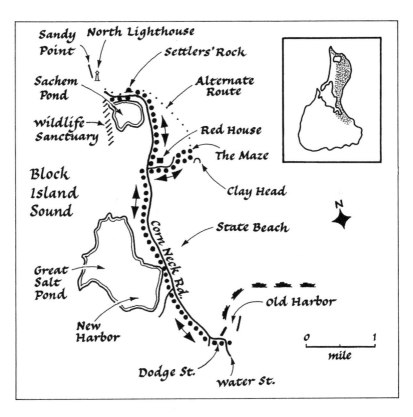

TRAIL

From the landing at Old Harbor, go right on Water Street, past the souvenir shops and the large wooden hotels that were built when New Shoreham was the "Bermuda of the North" at the turn of the century. Turn left on Dodge Street; then, at the island post office, turn right on Corn Neck Road and you are all set. Corn Neck Road runs all the way to Settlers' Rock at the island's northern tip.

You could also walk on the beach in this section—it's smooth sand for well over 1 mile—but this is a long walk and the sand may make you too weary too soon. The road is easier, even though you often have to contend with cars, mopeds, and bicycles headed for New Harbor or the state beach.

Shortly after you begin you will see one of the many historical monuments scattered around the island, this one noting the murder

183

of a Boston trader, John Oldham, by Indians in 1636. Historical insights make most walks more interesting, and Block Island has history all around.

You are soon able to see the masts of sailboats moored in Great Salt Pond to your left; then you will pass the state beach pavilion on your right. As you proceed, the views of the large pond improve, and in summer, when New Harbor is filled with boats (many of them large and luxurious), the panoramic vista is a delight for sailing enthusiasts.

Once past the pond, the road runs between old fields that have returned to bushes. There are some old farmhouses here and many new cottages, but the walk is usually uneventful for 1 mile or so. Still, it can be surprising. On one walk in this area, I found a yellow-headed blackbird, a species rare in New England and one I had never seen on mainland Rhode Island.

Rare birds seem drawn to Block Island, and each October birders from around the nation flock here. Many migratory birds use the island as a resting place, and seabirds that seldom visit the mainland seek refuge here during storms. The increase in birds, as well as the decrease in crowds and traffic, make autumn the ideal time to walk the island.

Settlers' Rock at the northern tip of Block Island lists the first permanent white inhabitants, who arrived in 1661.

About 3 miles from your start is a side road that runs to the ocean and The Maze, a privately owned thicket in which the owners have cut many miles of narrow, winding trails. If you so desire, you can spend an entire day wandering these trails; but if you also want to reach Settlers' Rock, it might be best simply to follow the trail that runs to Clay Head—a high cliff on the island's eastern shore—and take a brief look at The Maze, then return to the paved road. You could follow the shoreline left from Clay Head all the way to Settlers' Rock, but that will add considerable time and distance to your walk.

Finding The Maze has become easier. As you walk along Corn Neck Road, look for a signpost on the right indicating Clay Head Trail. It will be at a dirt road beside a red house at electrical pole No. 129. Follow the dirt road (off-limits to mopeds) a few hundred yards until it narrows to a footpath called Clay Head Nature Trail. Continue on the path as it passes an idyllic pond and then reaches the shore. You can go on down to the beach, a lovely spot with many boulders in the water and the clay cliffs looming above on the left, or you can turn left, following the nature trail; or you can do both.

If and when you take the nature trail, you'll soon see signs indicating that you are entering private property but that walkers are welcome. The paths off to the left of the nature trail are part of The Maze, the intricate network of paths created and maintained by the Lapham family. Take a little time to wander a few of the paths; you are likely to see and hear dozens of songbirds and perhaps spot a deer or two.

Back on Corn Neck Road the pavement rises, offering good views to the left of Block Island Sound. On a clear day, from the highest hilltop, you may be able to see (on your left) Gardiner's Island and Fisher's Island, part of New York State, as well as some of the Connecticut shoreline. Ahead is mainland Rhode Island, and off to your right is the Massachusetts shore—four states from one vantage point.

There are a few taller trees lining the road as you head downhill. In minutes you will arrive at Sachem Pond, a picturesque pond that, along with the rugged dunes on the opposite shore, makes up a wildlife refuge. The dunes are the nesting site of numerous gulls, terns, and other birds.

Corn Neck Road ends at Settlers' Rock, a monument on the northern end of Sachem Pond. The rock commemorates the arrival, in 1661, of the 16 Boston men who became the first permanent white inhabitants of the island. Near the rock, which is about 5 miles from your start counting the walk along Clay Head Trail to The Maze, are picnic tables and a small beach on the pond side, making it an excellent place to rest.

The ambitious can continue, however, as a sandy lane runs farther out on the point, to North Lighthouse, a nonoperating landmark. Beyond the light is Sandy Point, a narrow, sometimes submerged sandbar that has been the scene of a great many shipwrecks over the centuries.

Sooner or later, though, you will have to leave this alluring place and head back toward the ferry. Keep in mind that it's a 4-mile walk from Settlers' Rock. Make sure you give yourself enough time. The one thing you don't want to do on Block Island is hurry.

More from The Countryman Press and Backcountry Publications

Guides from our Walks & Rambles Series:
More Walks & Rambles in Rhode Island
Walks & Rambles on Cape Cod & the Islands
Walks & Rambles in Dutchess and Putnam Counties
Walks in Nature's Empire

Explorer's Guides:
Cape Cod and the Islands: An Explorer's Guide
Connecticut: An Explorer's Guide
The Hudson Valley and Catskill Mountains: An Explorer's Guide
Maine: An Explorer's Guide
Massachusetts: An Explorer's Guide
New Hampshire: An Explorer's Guide
Rhode Island: An Explorer's Guide
Vermont: An Explorer's Guide

New England Guides from our Biking Series:
25 Bicycle Tours in Maine
30 Bicycle Tours in New Hampshire
25 Mountain Bike Tours in Massachusetts
25 Mountain Bike Tours in Vermont

New England Guides from our Hiking Series:
Fifty Hikes in Connecticut
Fifty Hikes in Massachusetts
Fifty Hikes in Northern Maine
Fifty Hikes in Southern Maine
Fifty Hikes in Vermont
Fifty Hikes in the White Mountains
Fifty More Hikes in New Hampshire

Also:
Canoeing Massachusetts, Rhode Island, and Massachusetts
Canoe Camping Vermont & New Hampshire Rivers

Our books are available through bookstores, or they may be ordered directly from the publisher. VISA/Mastercard accepted. For ordering information or for a complete catalog, please contact:

The Countryman Press, Inc.
P.O. Box 175
Woodstock, VT 05091-0175
(800) 245-4151